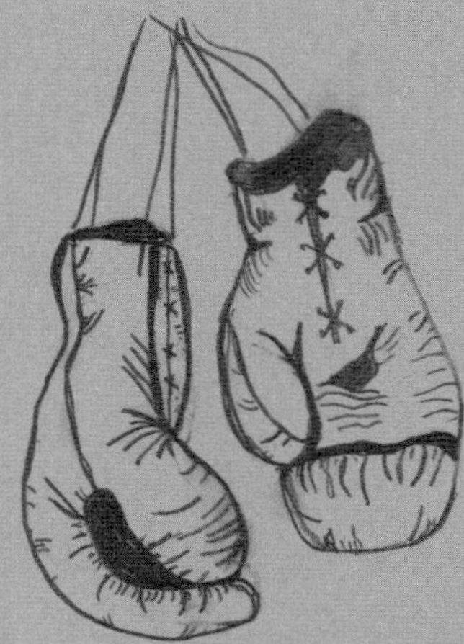

Fight!

The brilliant boxer is an artist, albeit in an art not readily comprehensible, or palatable, to most observers. The instruments of his art are his own and his opponent's bodies. That it is, in a sense, a contemplative art — contemplated, dreamt-of, for weeks, months, even years before it is executed — is a proposition important to understand if one is to understand the boxer.

Joyce Carol Oates,
On Boxing

THE MODERN KIDS

JONA FRANK

Introduction by Bruce Weber

KEHRER

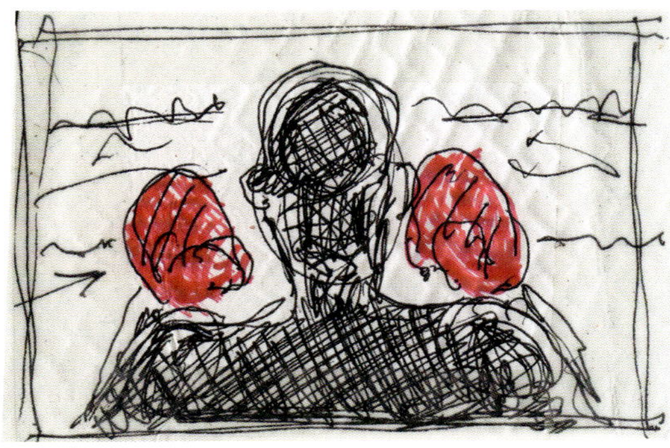

For Patrick

For understanding why I was gripped.
For always understanding.

GLORY

When I get to a new town, be it in Ireland or Wales, France or Thailand, the first thing I do is go to a boxing gym. I try to meet the trainer and a couple of his guys, because they give me the "real deal" of what the city might be like. No matter where the gym is, I always encounter a lot of people I want to put into my photographs. Jona really picked the right place. There's something about gyms in America these days that has become too commercial – they're all cleaned up, bright and fancy. Jona found a place with lots of dirt and soul.

As you enter a boxing gym, you step into a world that isn't just about the sport. A father watches his son spar. One of the trainers tells an amazing fight story. Boxing gyms are full of blood and guts and great sayings on the walls. There is such a mixture of pain and joy – it's just like growing up.

When I first looked at these pictures, I asked Nan, "What's this woman like?" I had a feeling about her after seeing the work – how she might look, what her voice and hand gestures might be like. I was curious about her because of the people she chose to photograph and how she made the pictures. That was a thrill. It's like we'd met in a pub somewhere and shared a few beers. I felt like she was a buddy. That's what is so great about photography and filmmaking – you get a sense of the person behind the camera right away.

In Jona's pictures of young boxers, I feel like I am actually looking at little old men, old souls before their time, guys who already have a history in living. So much of their stories are written in their faces, in their scars, in their ears – everything. Jona gets to this crazy level of emotion and intimacy that most photographers hope for with the people in front of their camera.

Her photographs and film are a poem about memory – lost and regained – a record of these men's lives. If I talk to her about them twenty years from now, I'd imagine it will be even more "to the heart."

Jona's work brings back so many incredible memories of my time making the film *Broken Noses* with Andy Minsker. Andy was the driving force, a beautiful character then and now. It's kind of hard to think of that time because it was so emotional for all of us involved. For the film's poster, we included a line that Andy said about boxing: "It makes men of them fast." But what does it mean to be a man? What does it mean to be a boxer? I look at the guys in Jona's pictures and find myself asking the same questions. Like Andy, it wasn't so important for Jona's guys if they won or lost the title – but it meant everything when they could "man up" and accept life with a handshake.

Although some of the most gentlemanly people I have ever met are boxers, for Jona to go into a boxing gym as a woman is a very rare thing. I used to visit a gym out in Las Vegas called Johnny Tocco's that had a sign which read, "No Women Allowed." But Jona's boxers let her have this experience. They wanted to share their moment of glory with her, and she in turn made heroes of them in her photographs. These pictures will be placed on the mantles and the walls in their homes. People will take notice. Their hard work will matter.

Some people might confuse the realism of Jona's work with a certain anti-romanticism. But she's just bending the ideal by holding true to the photographer's mantra: "Keep your eyes open and be true to your heart."

— Bruce Weber, New York, 2015

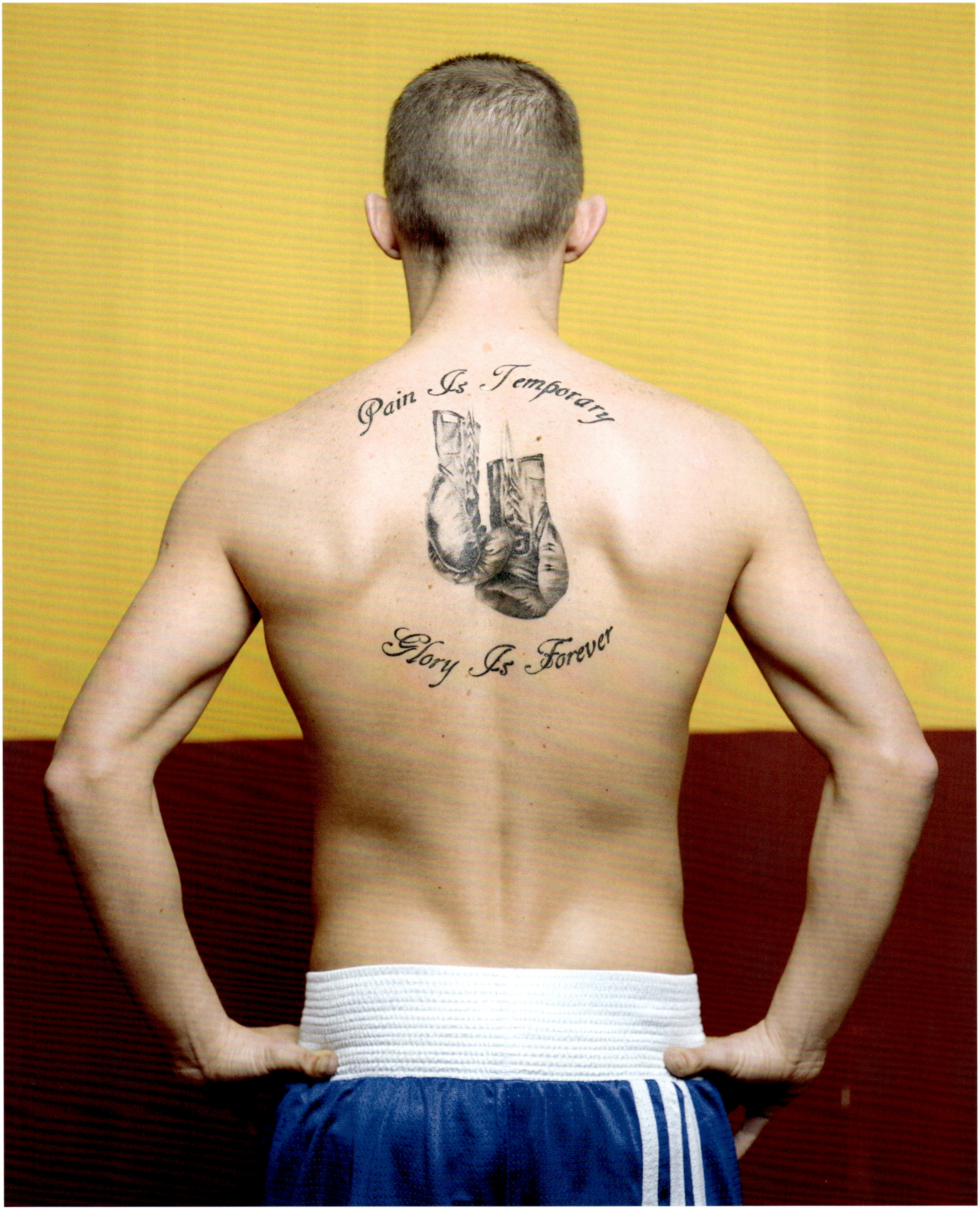
Pain Is Temporary
Glory Is Forever

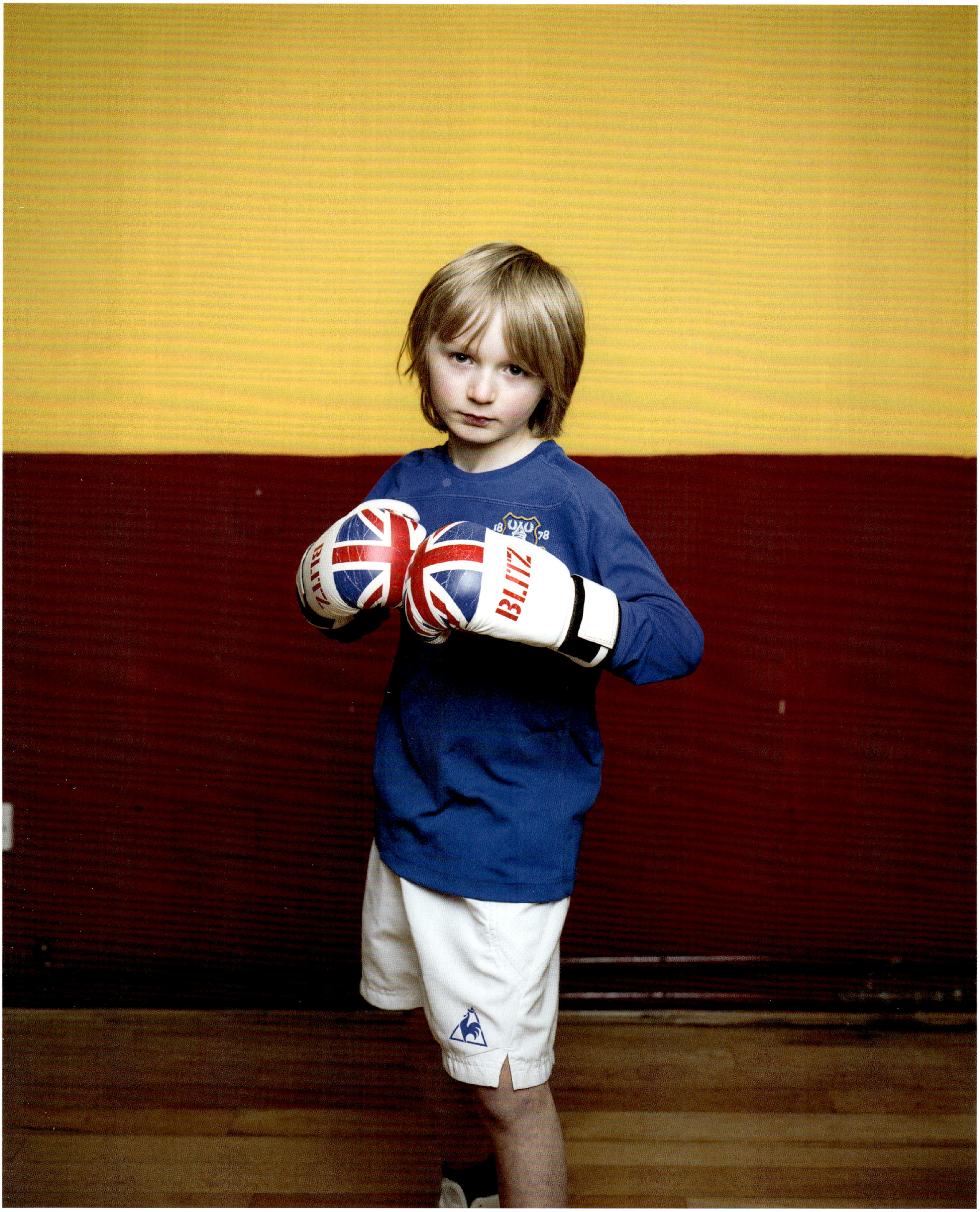
BLITZ

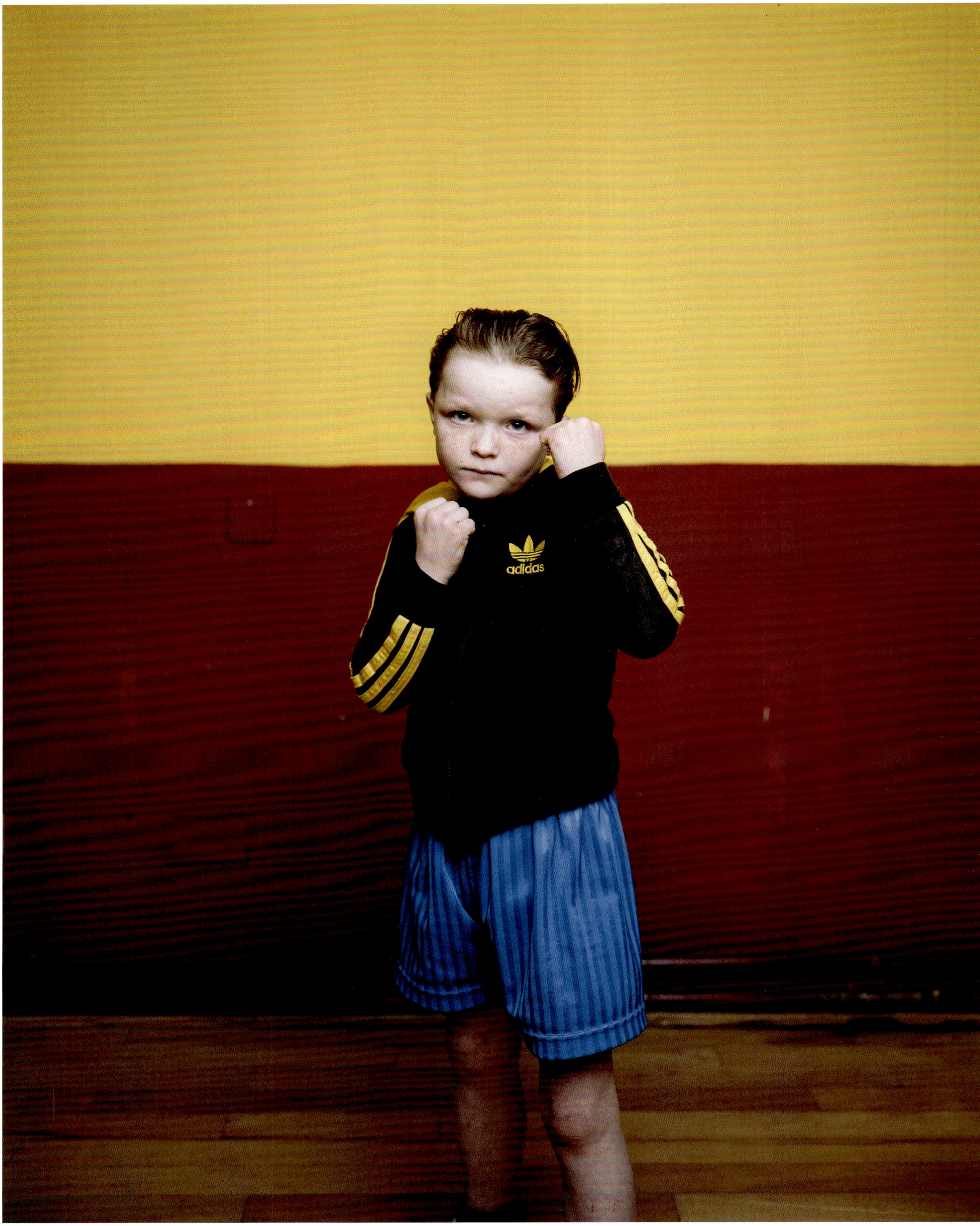
adidas

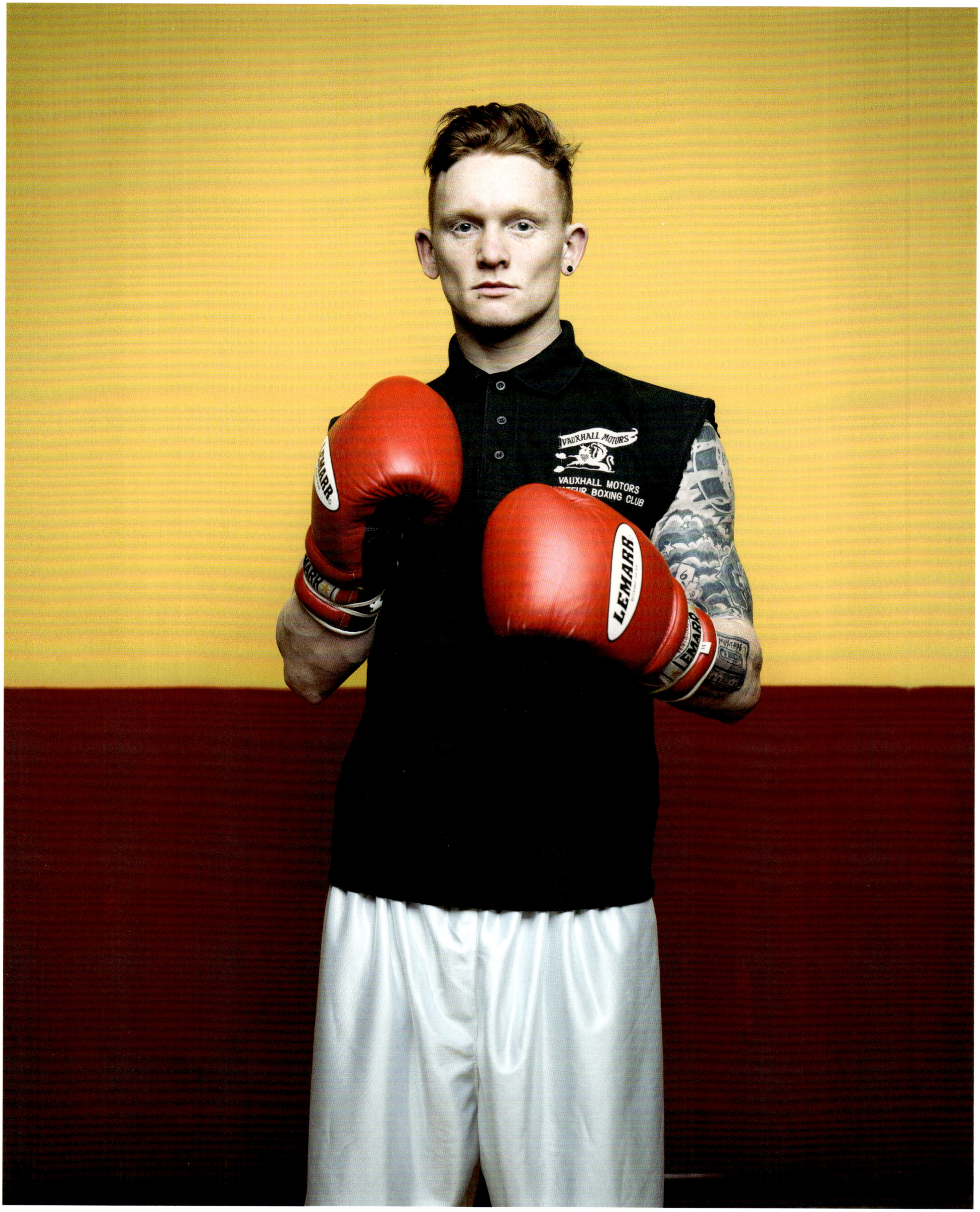
VAUXHALL MOTORS
VAUXHALL MOTORS
BOXING CLUB
LEMARR
LEMARR

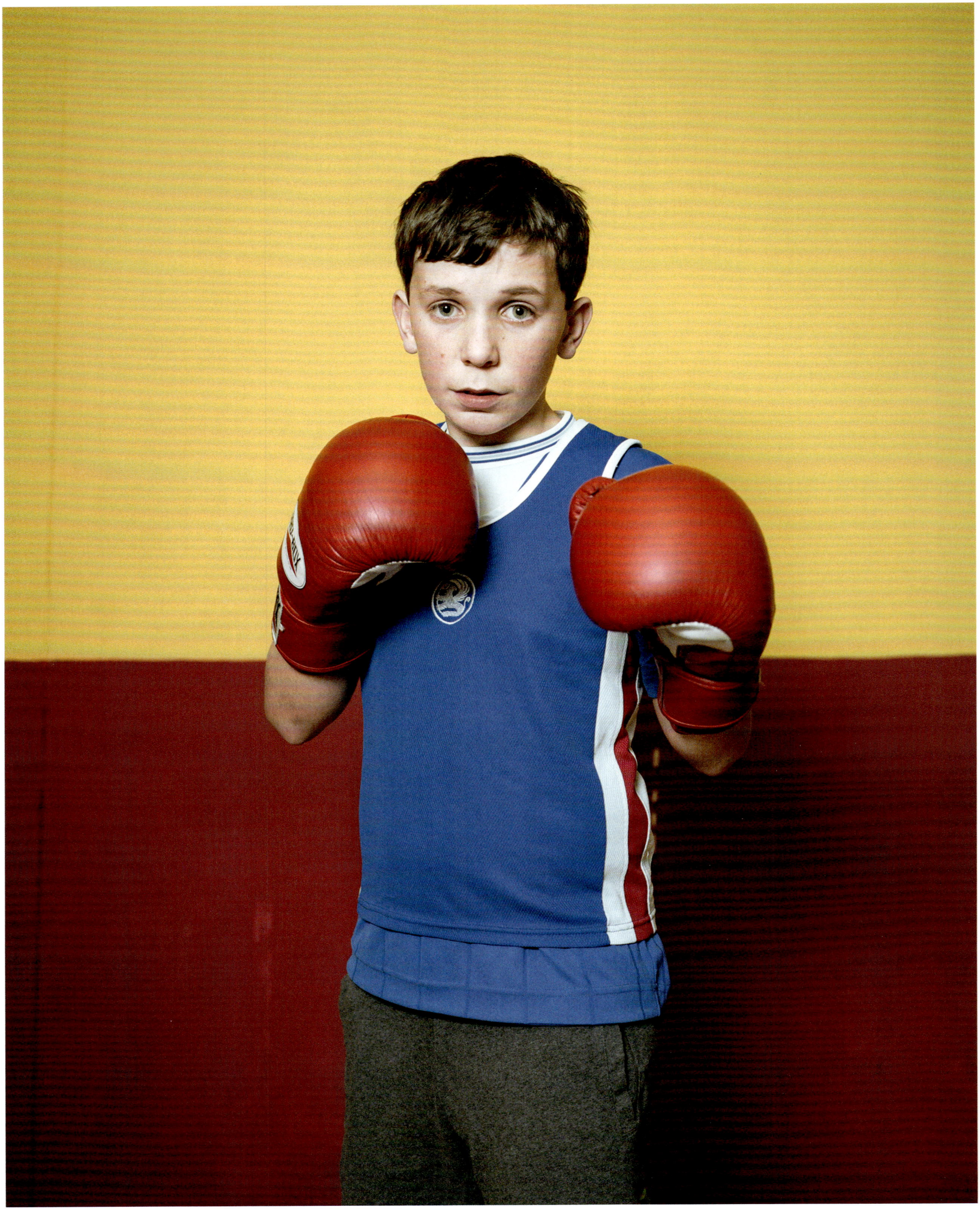

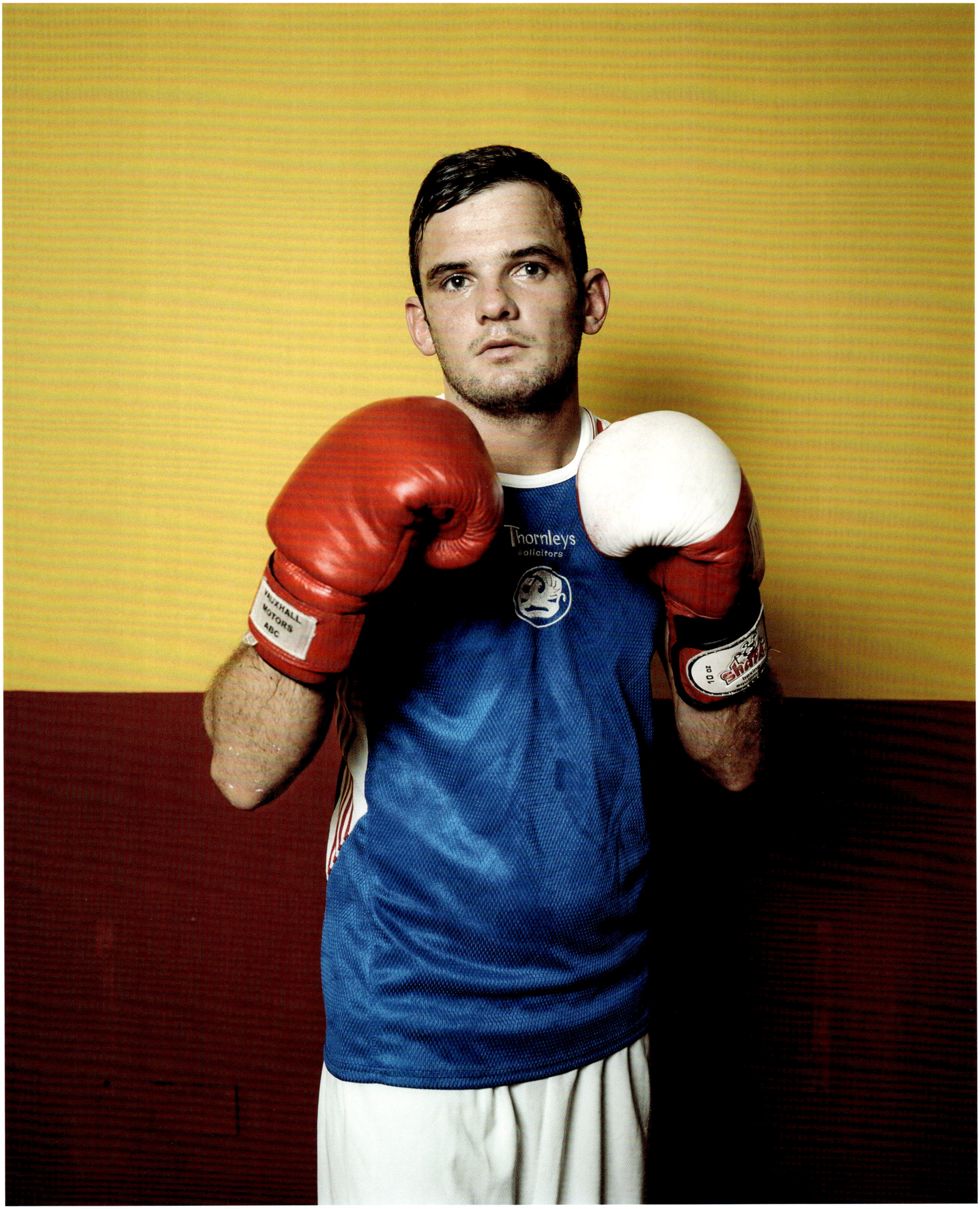
Thornleys
solicitors
VAUXHALL
MOTORS
ABC
10 oz

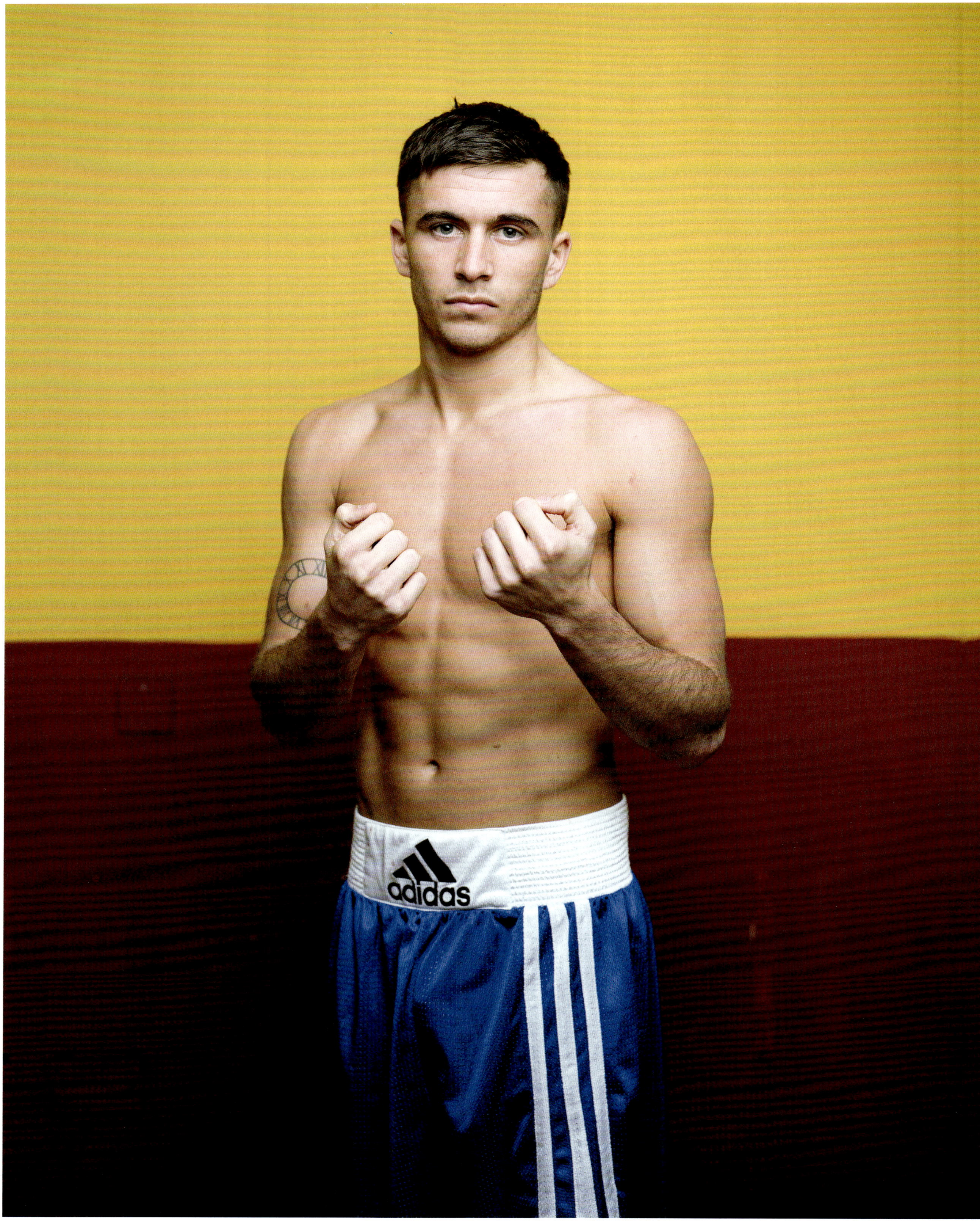
adidas

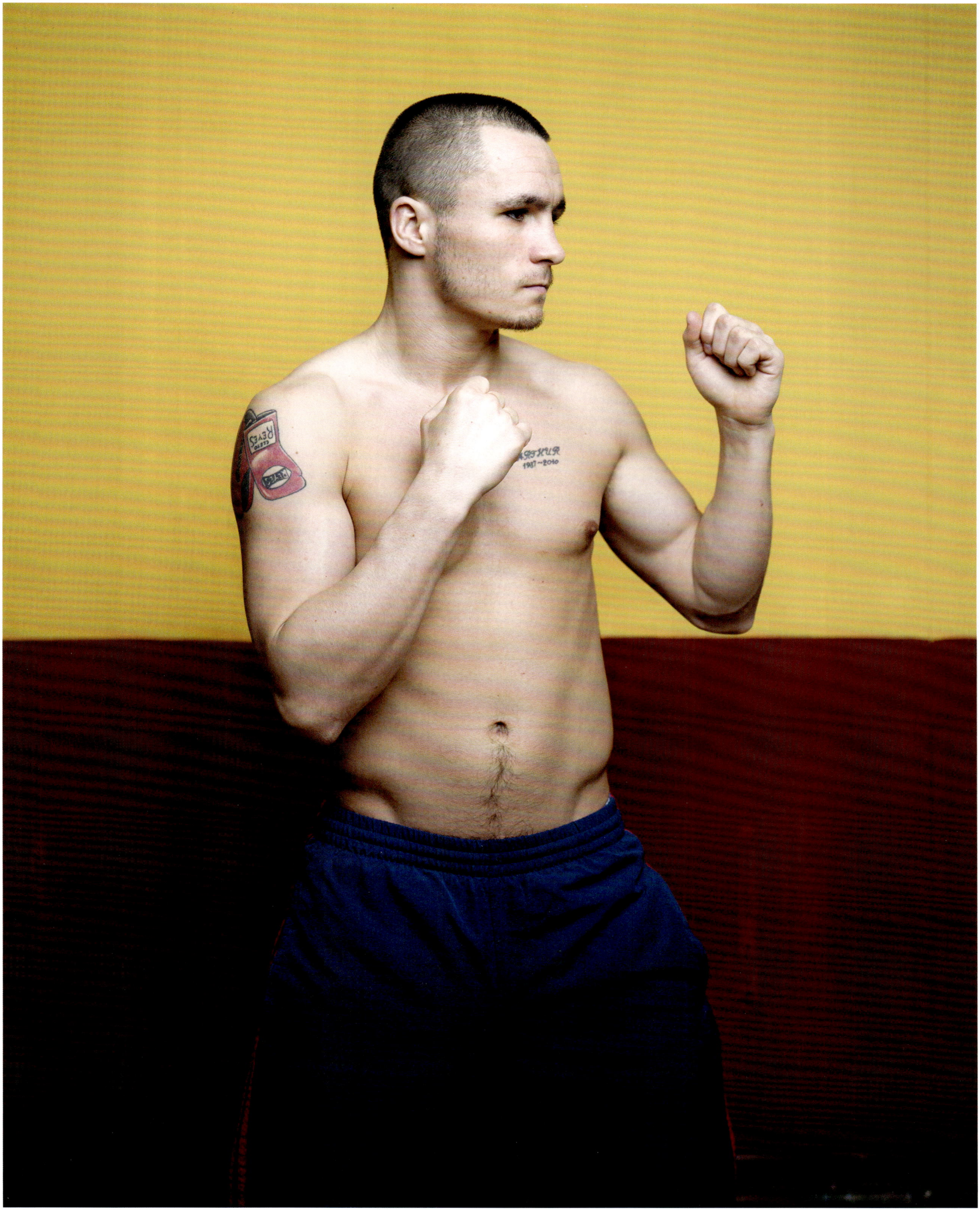

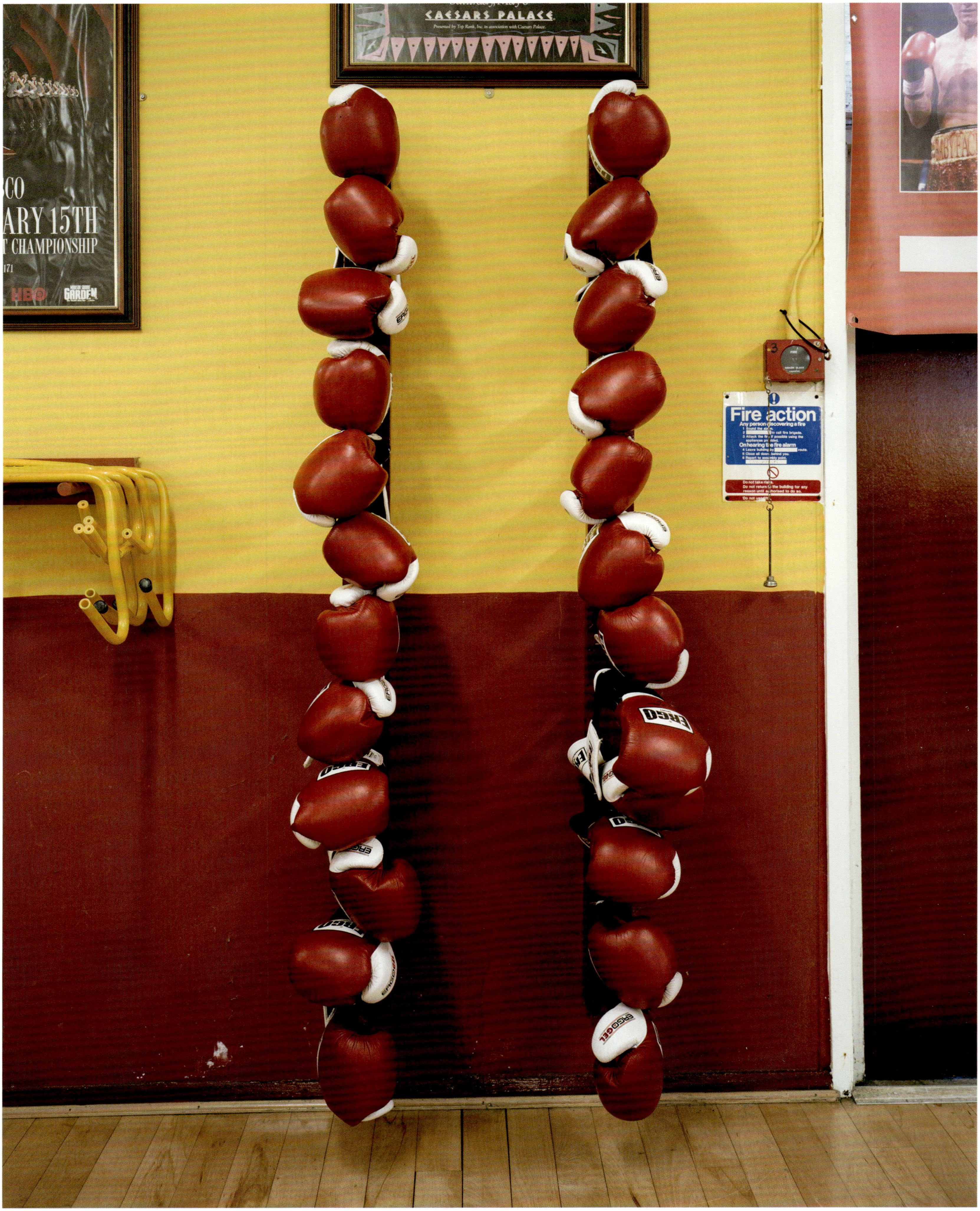
CAESARS PALACE
CHAMPIONSHIP
HBO
Fire action
Any person discovering a fire
On hearing the fire alarm
ERGO
ERGO GEL

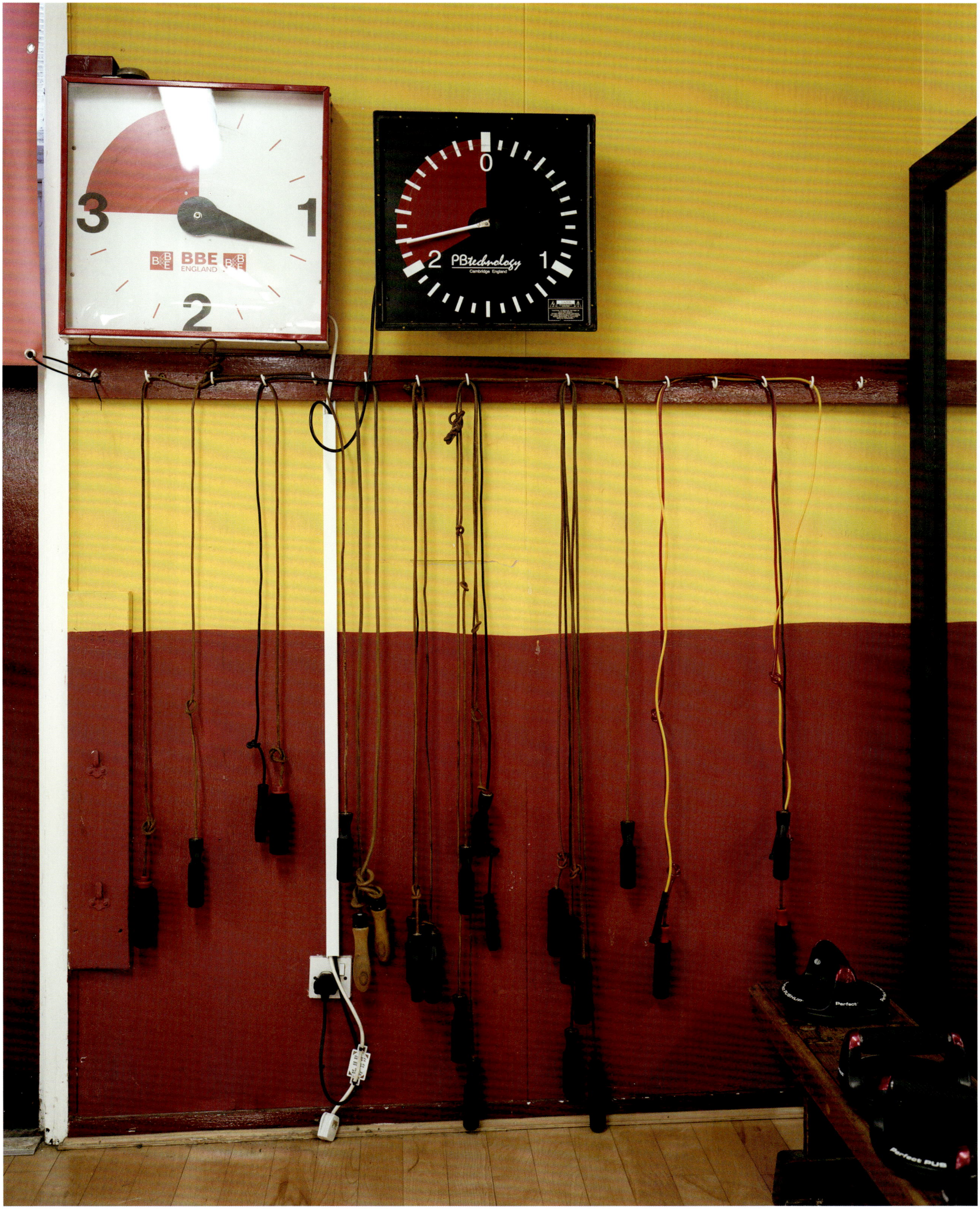
3
1
BBE
ENGLAND
2
0
2
PBtechnology
Cambridge England
1
Perfect
Perfect PUS

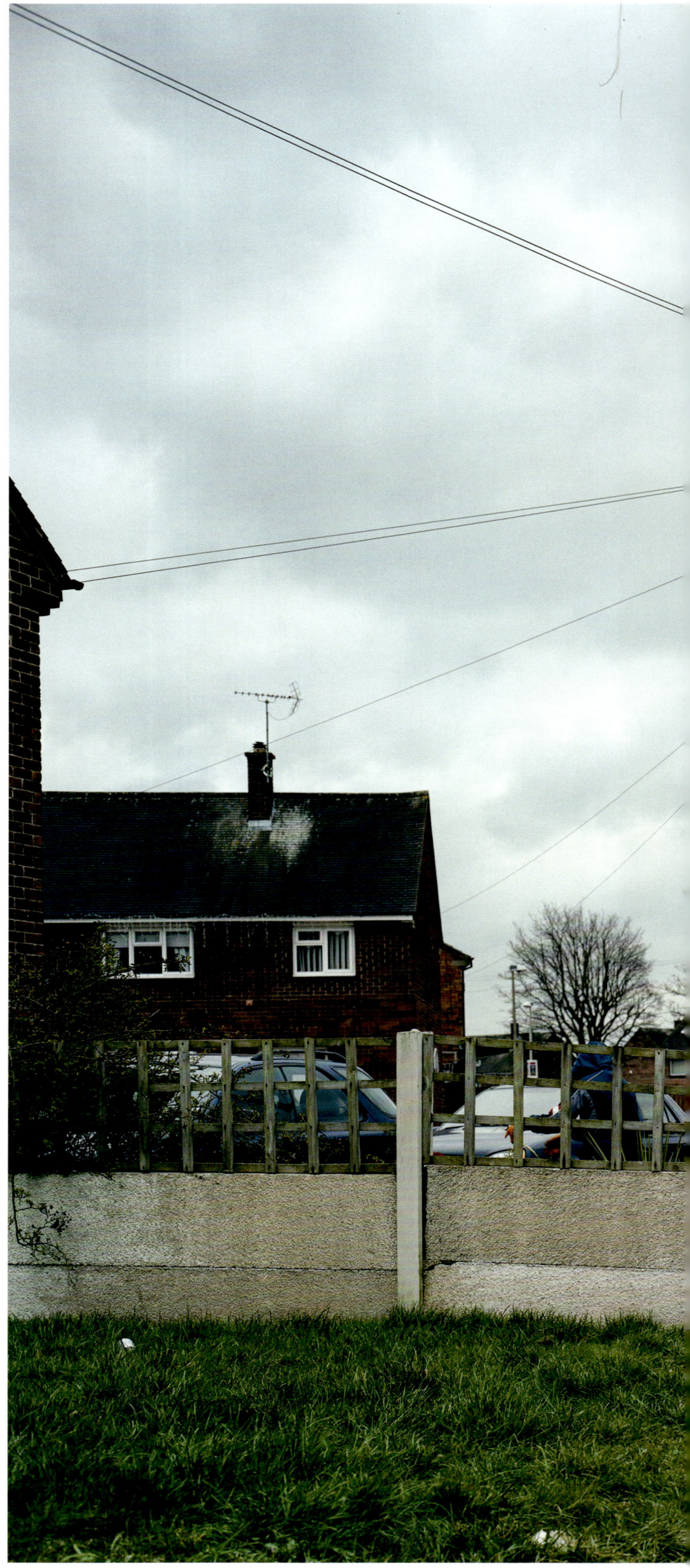

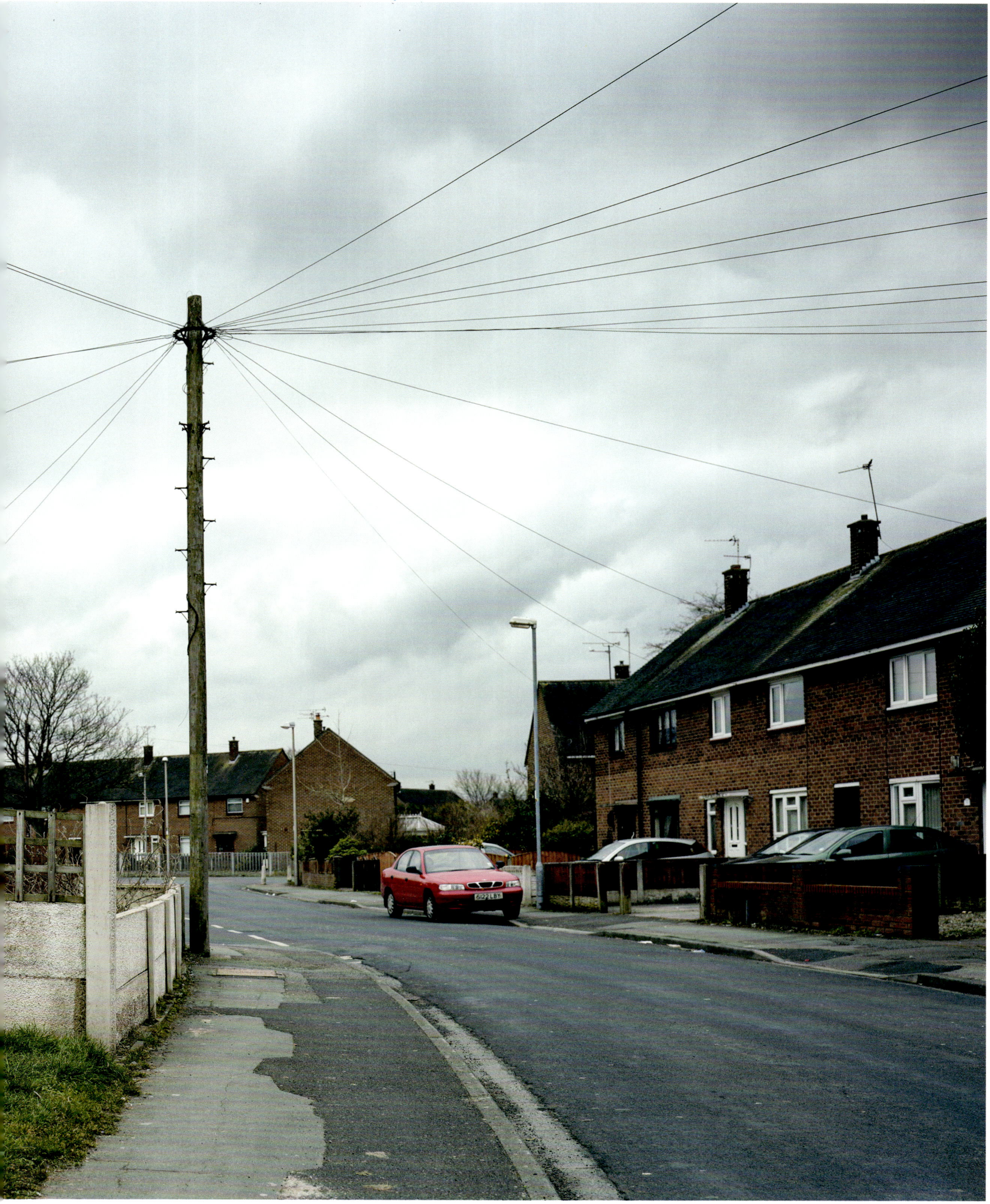

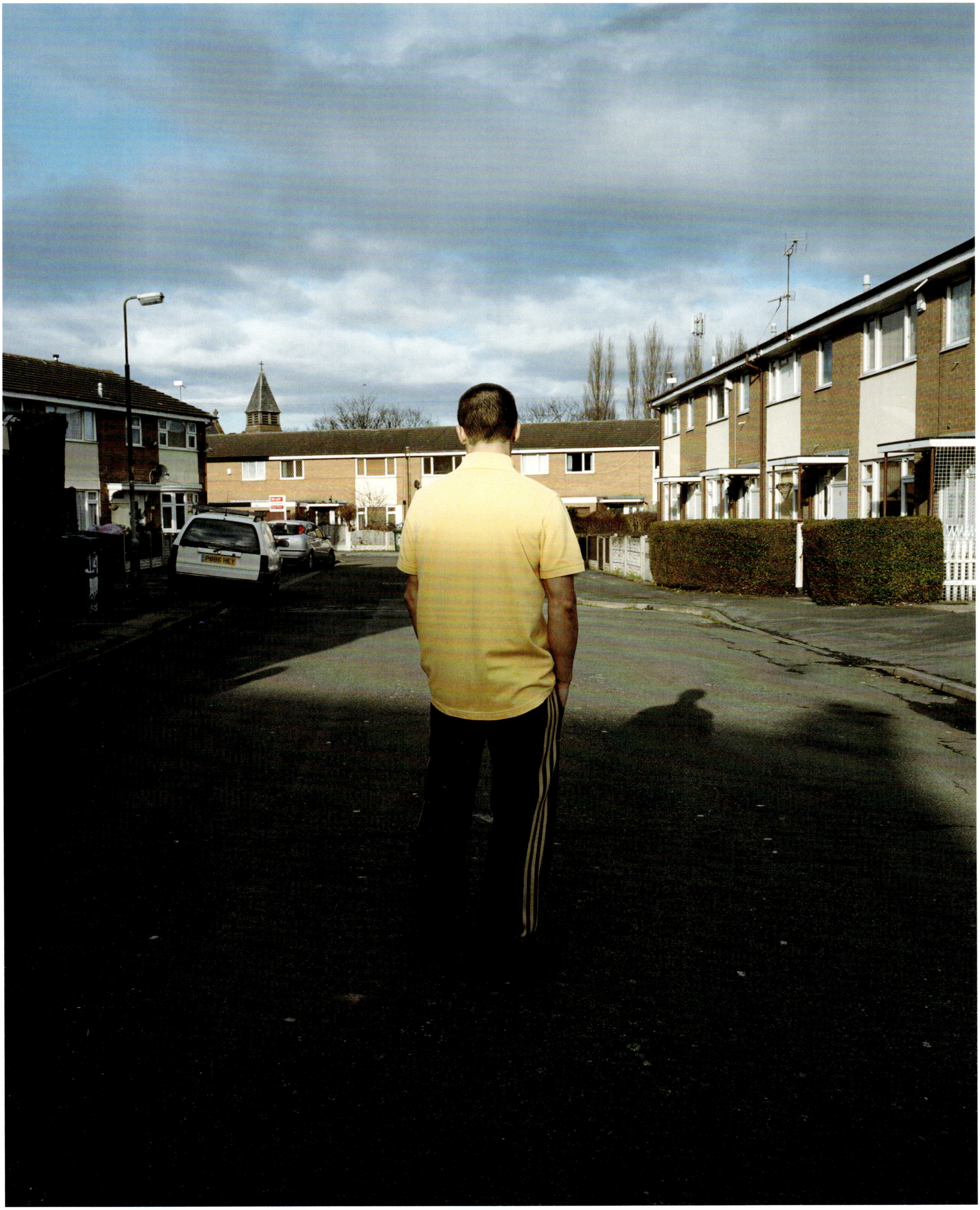

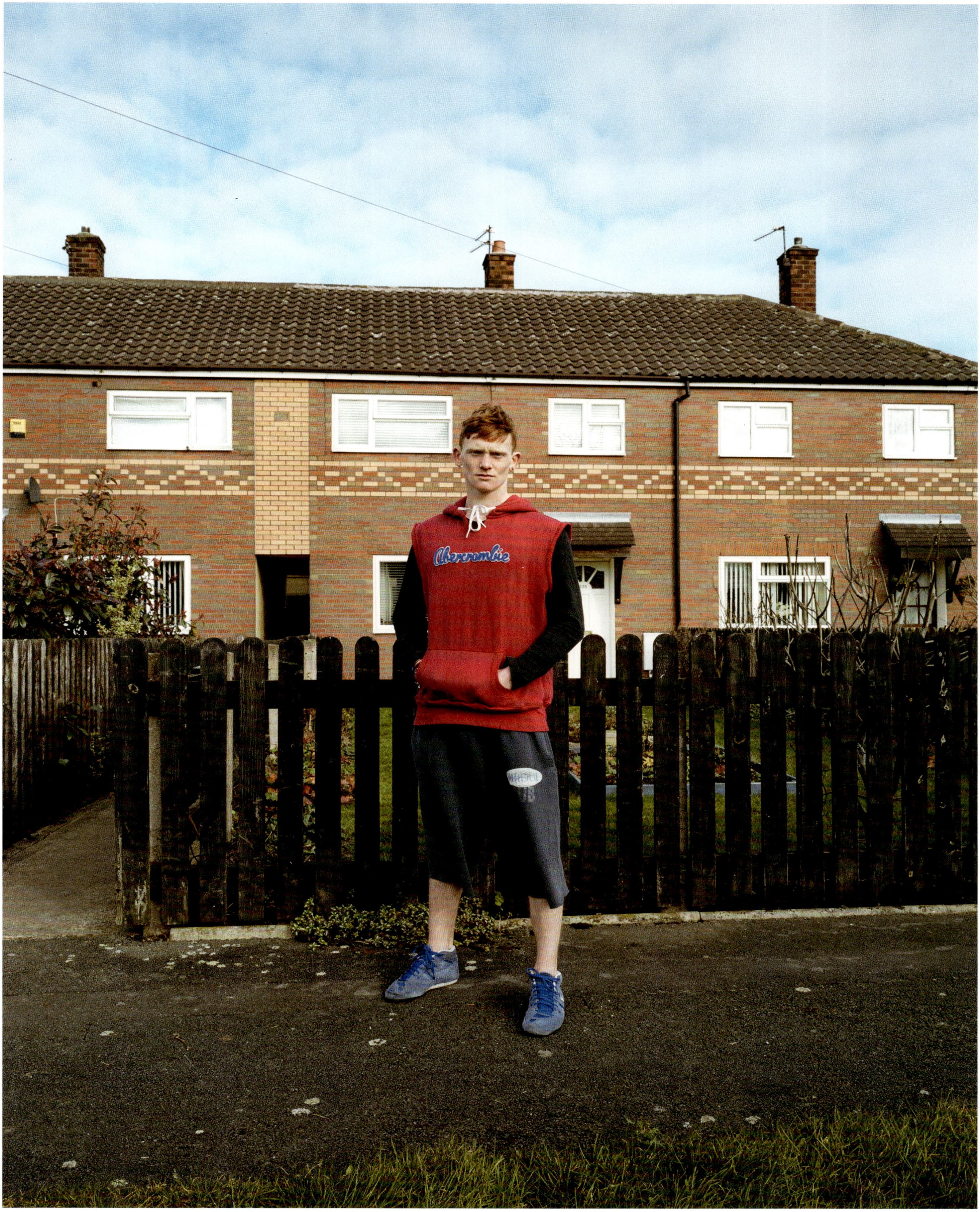
Abercrombie

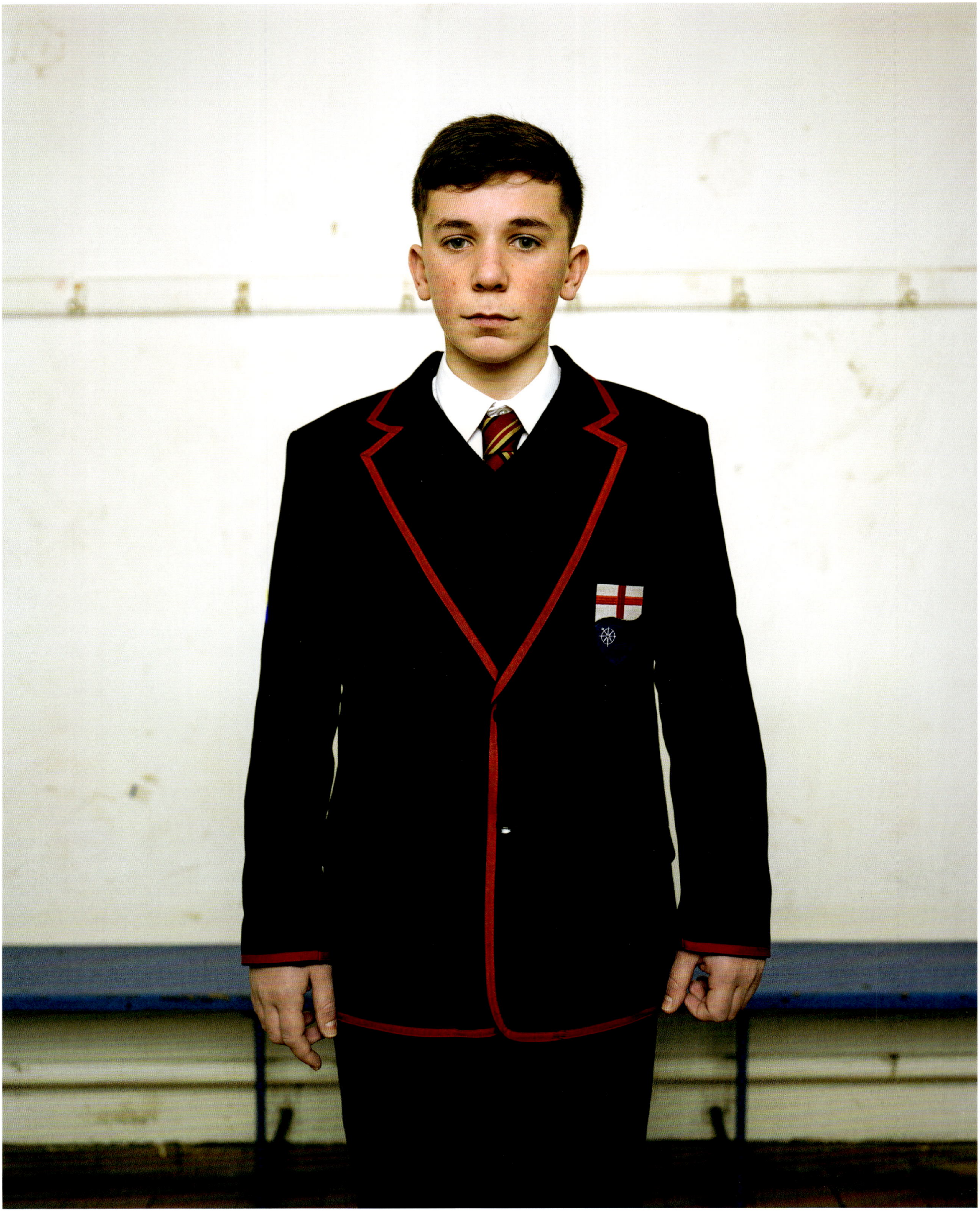

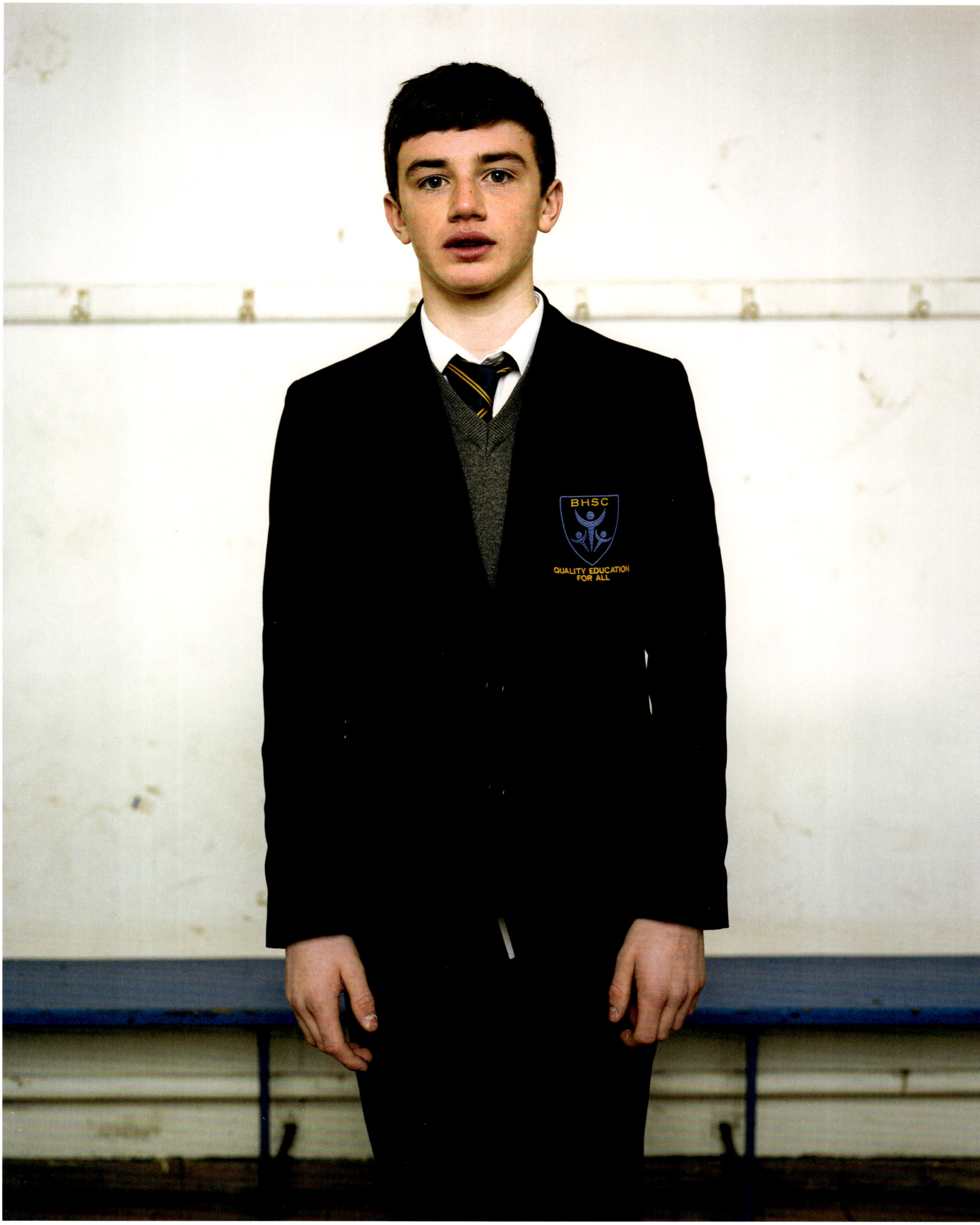
BHSC
QUALITY EDUCATION
FOR ALL

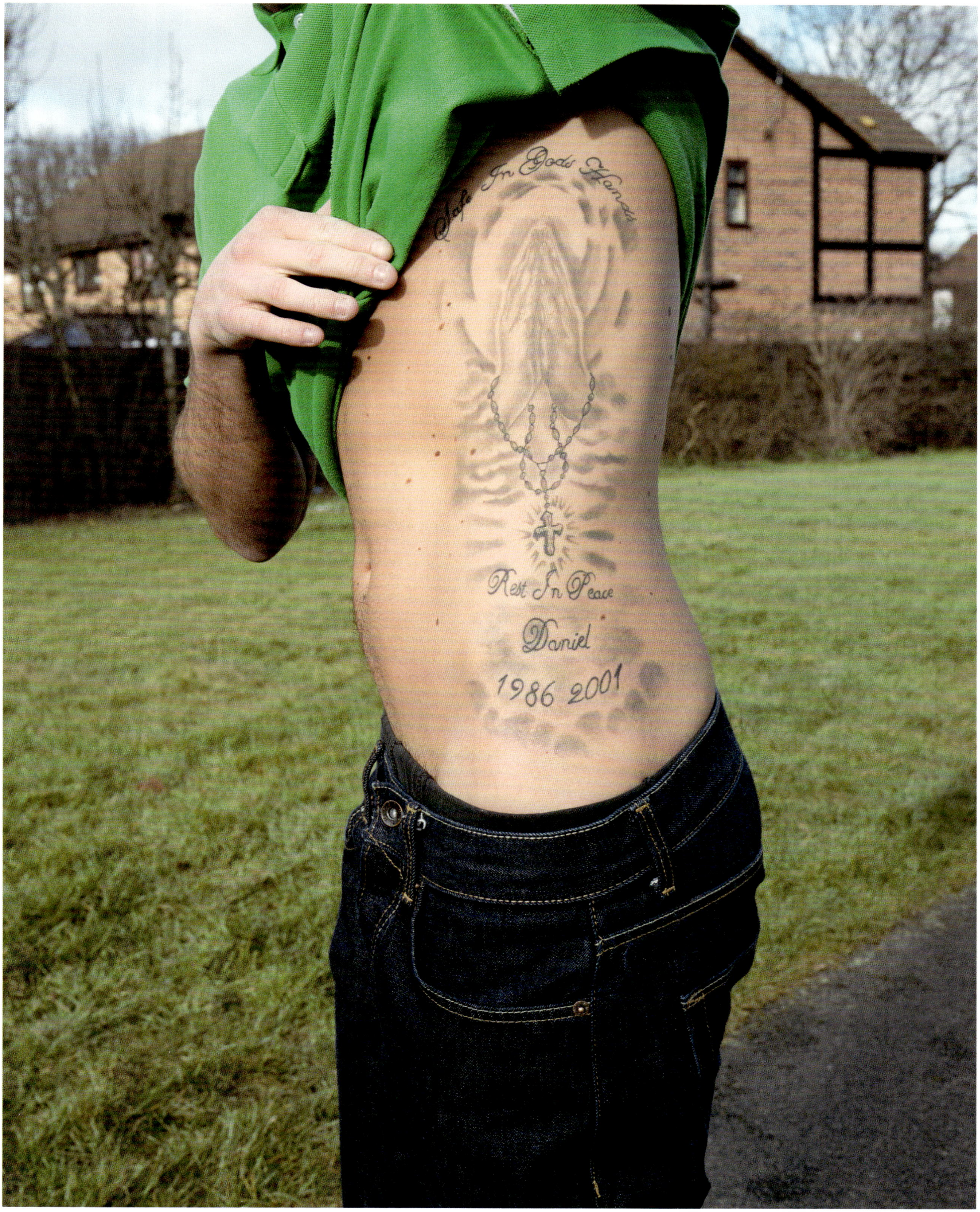
Safe In Gods Hands
Rest In Peace
Daniel
1986 2001

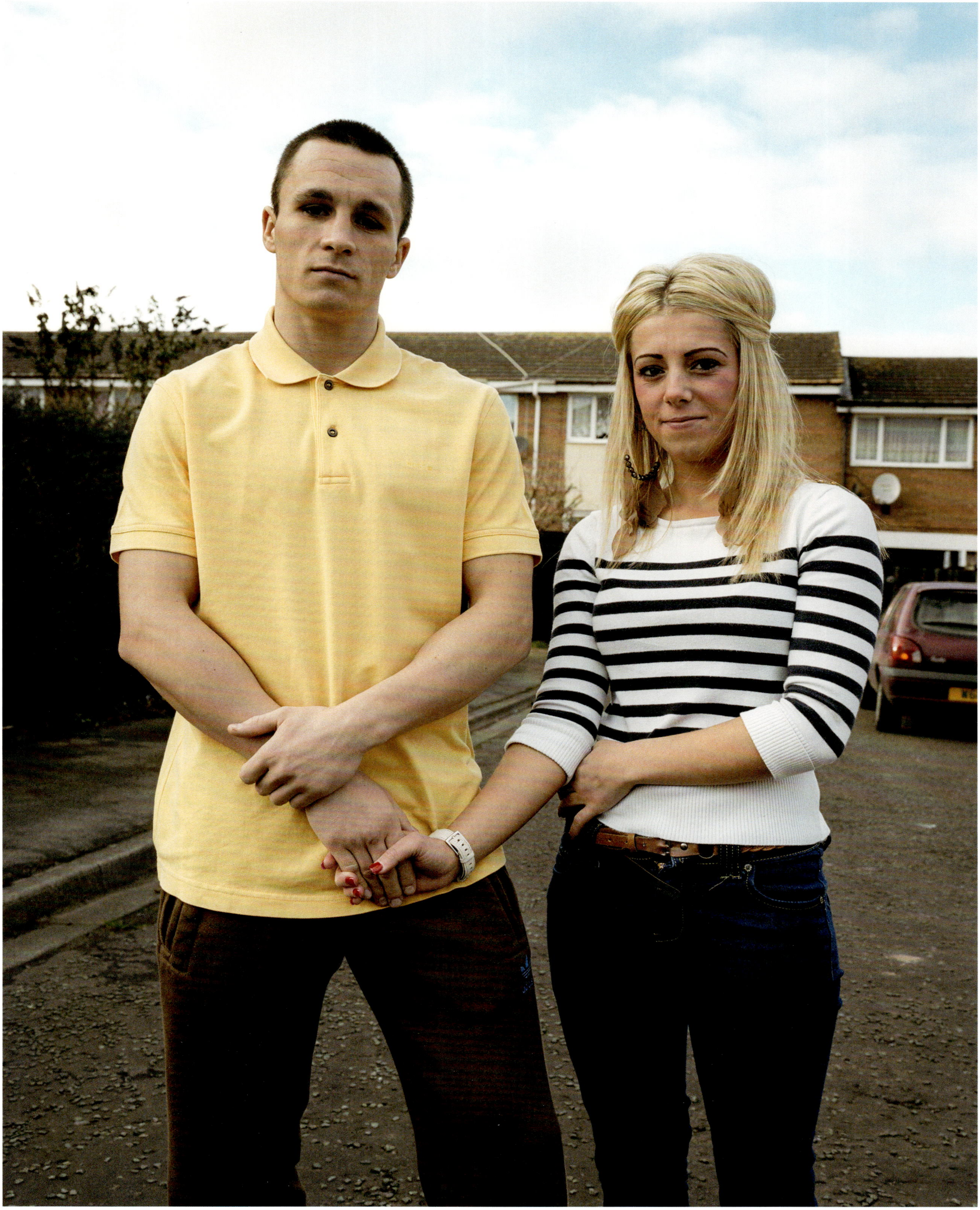

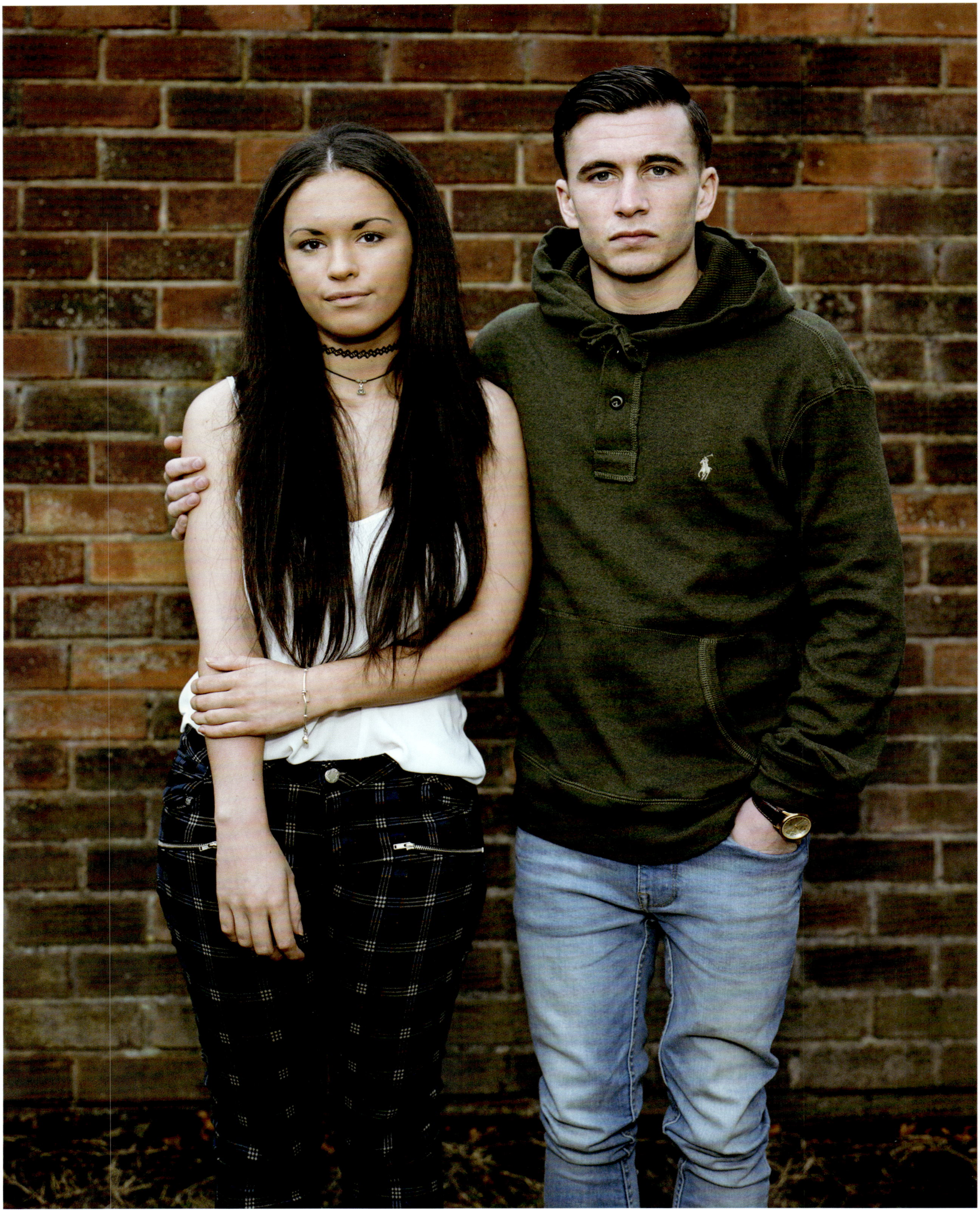

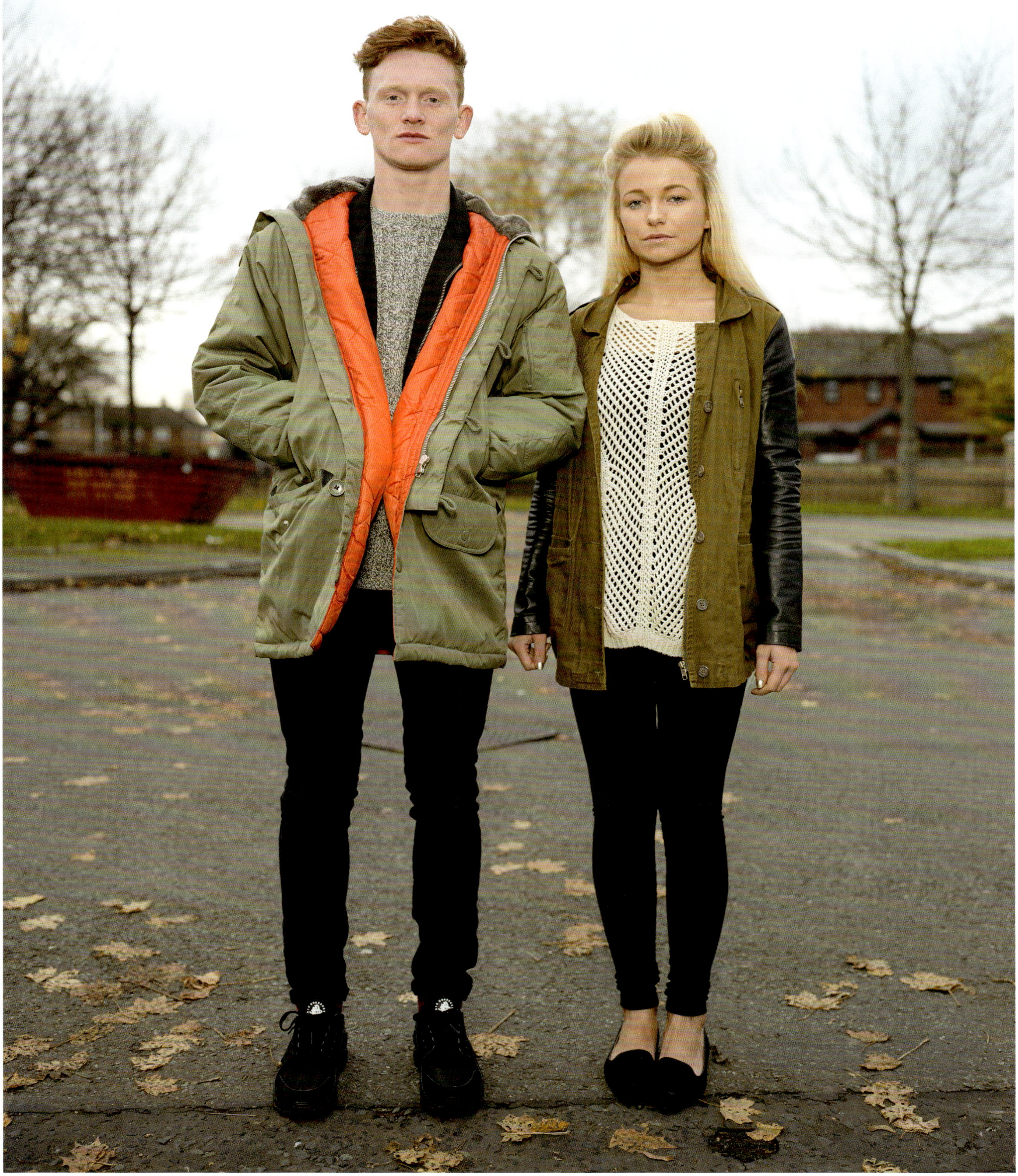

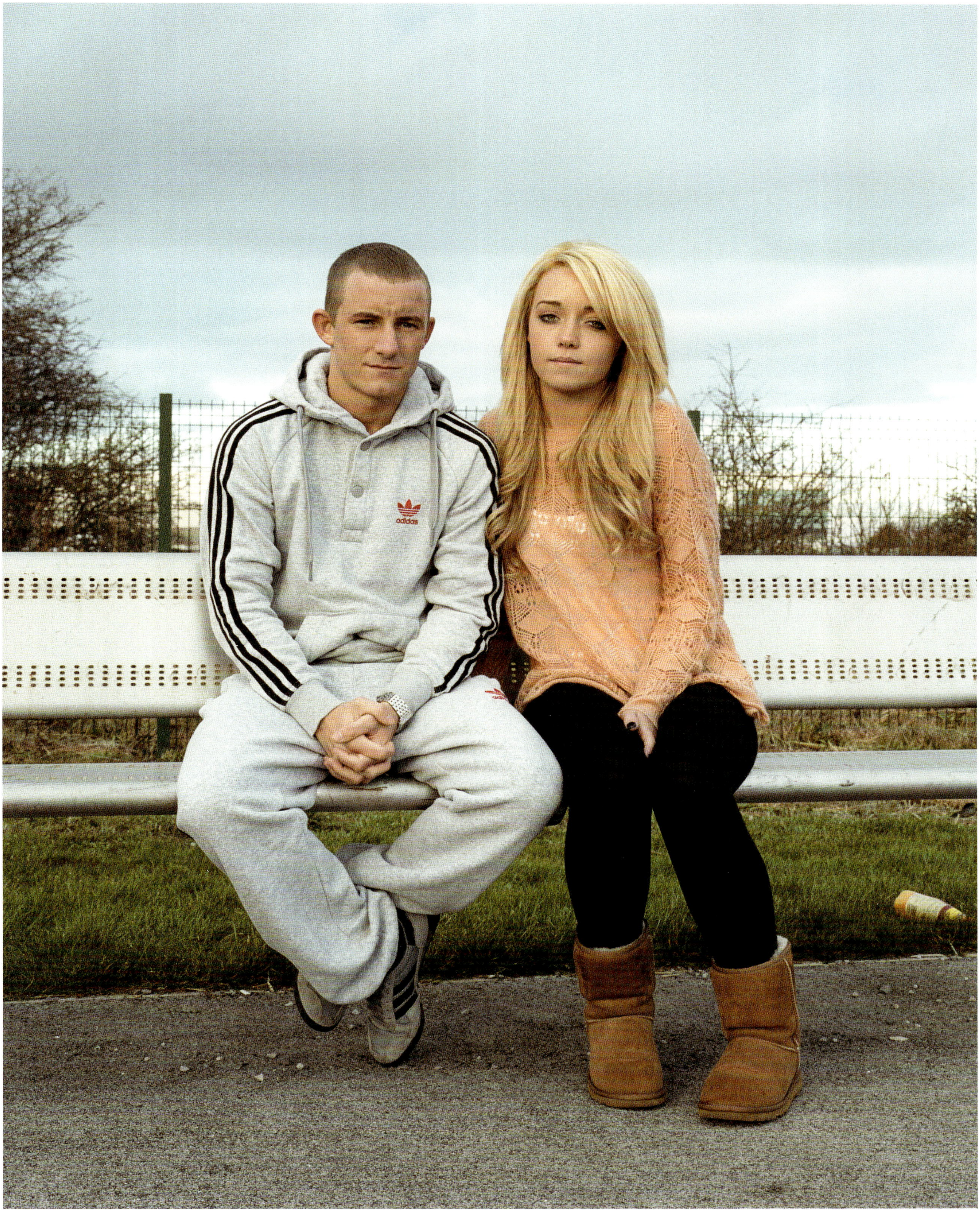

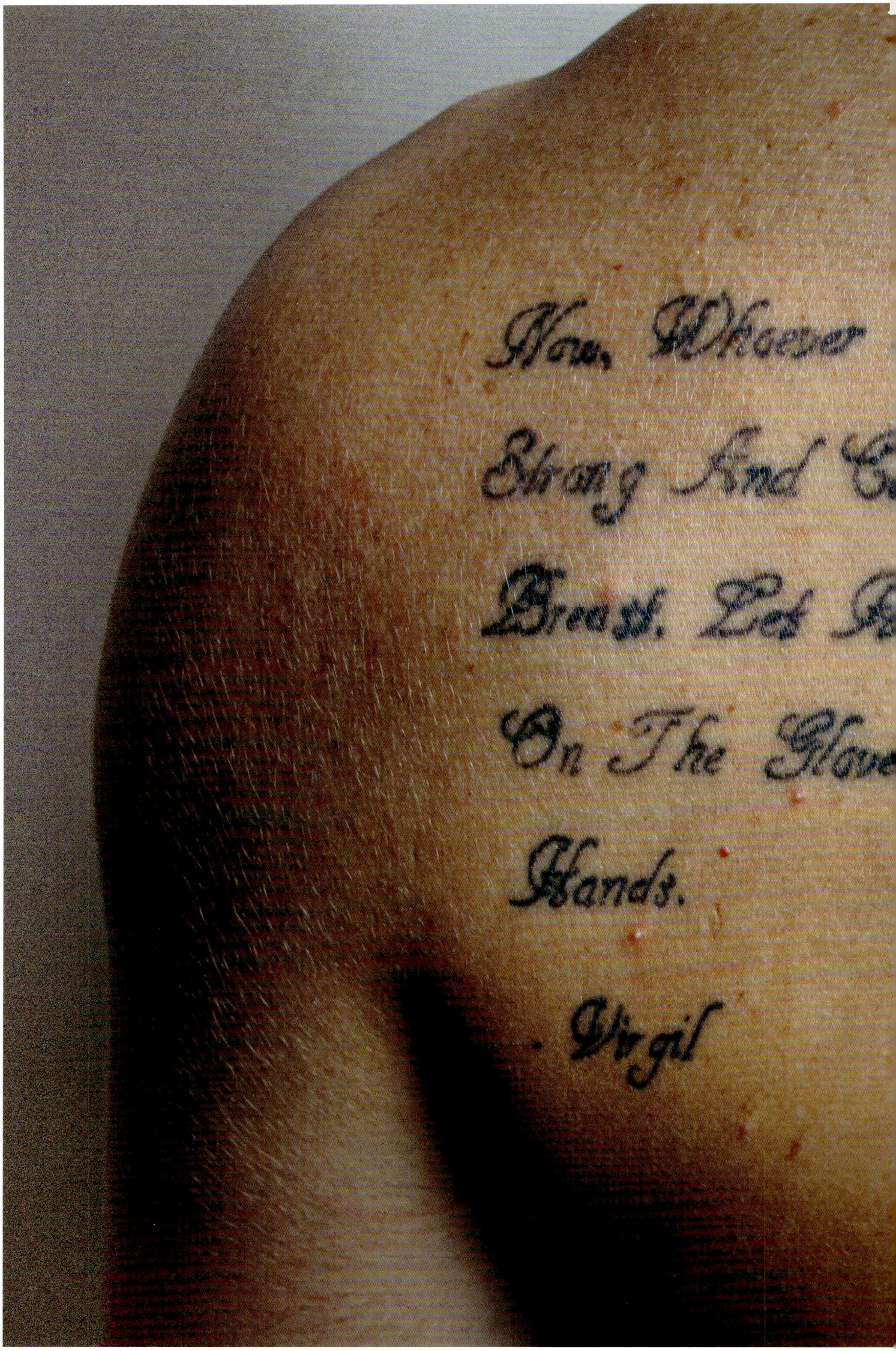
Now, Whoever
Strong And
Breast, Let
On The
Hands.
Virgil

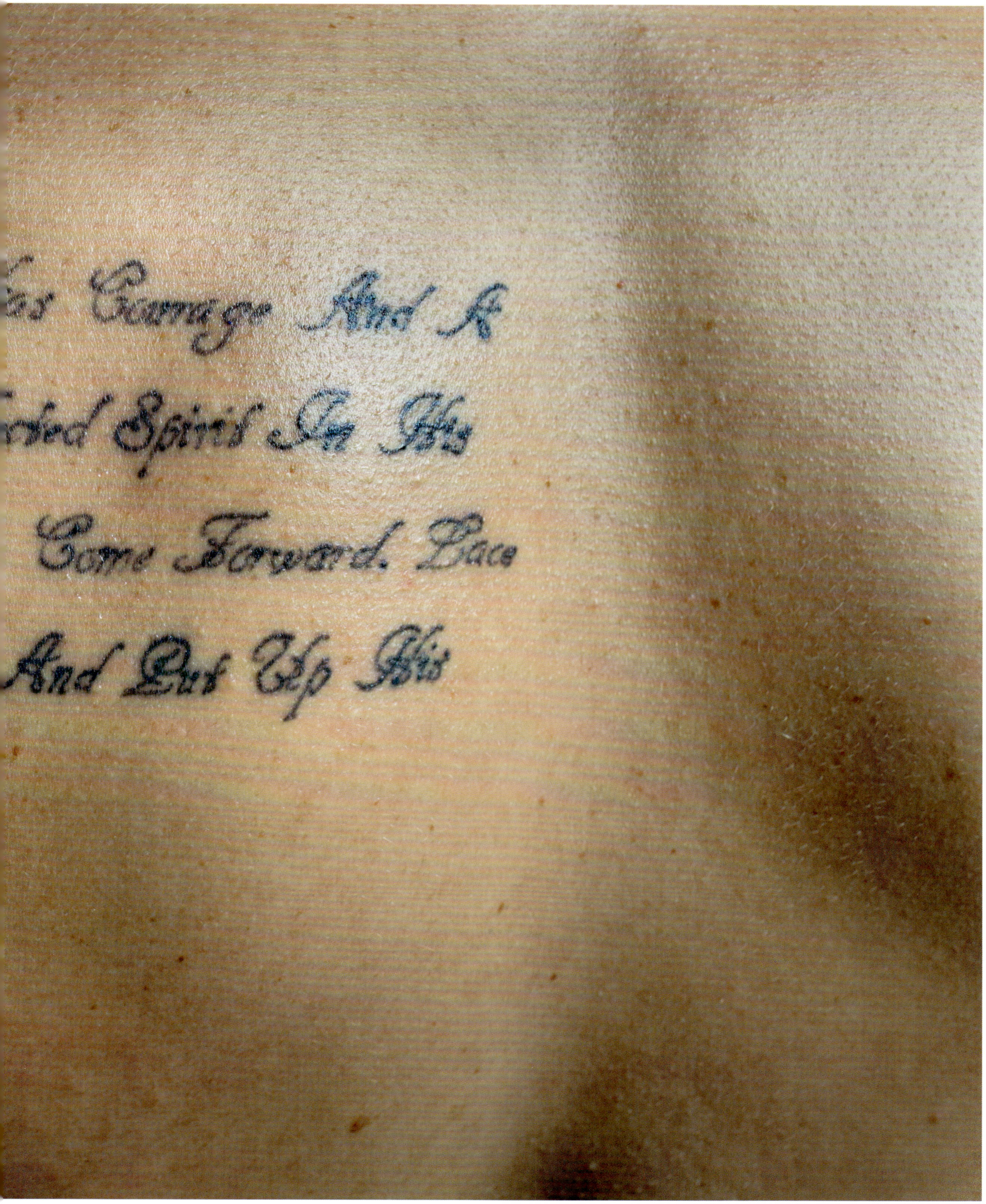
Courage And A
Spirit In His
Come Forward. Place
And Put Up His

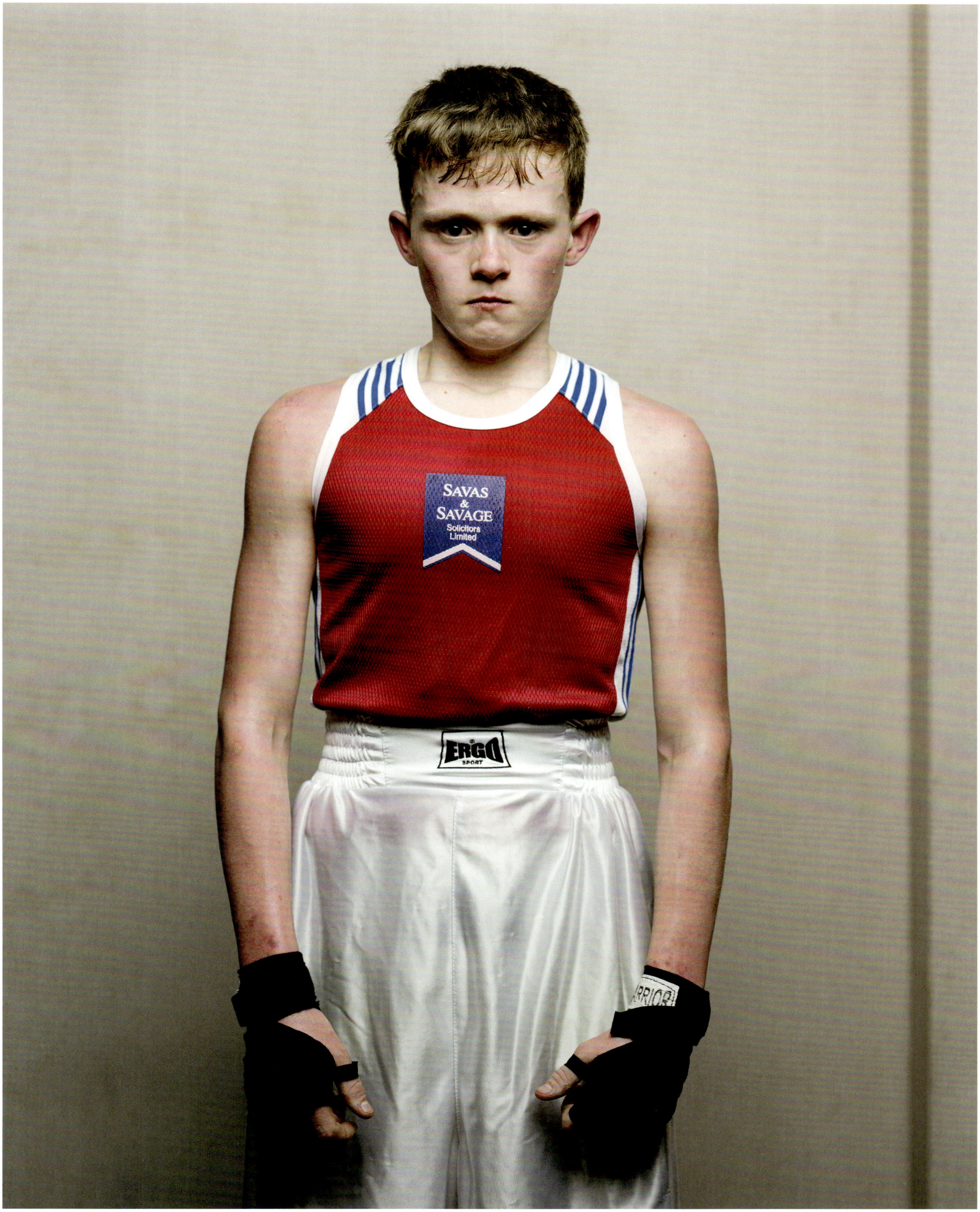
SAVAS
&
SAVAGE
Solicitors
Limited
ERGO
SPORT

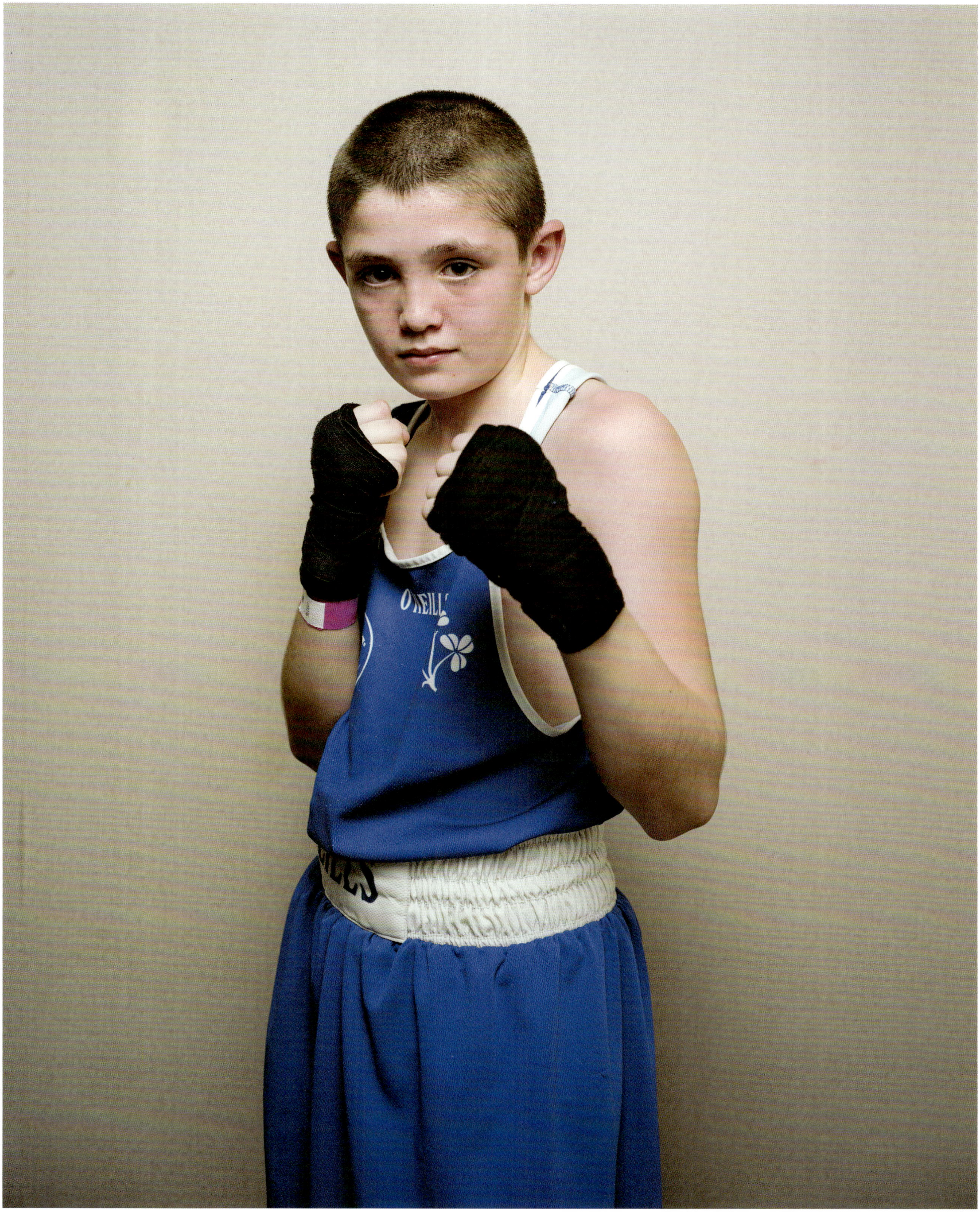

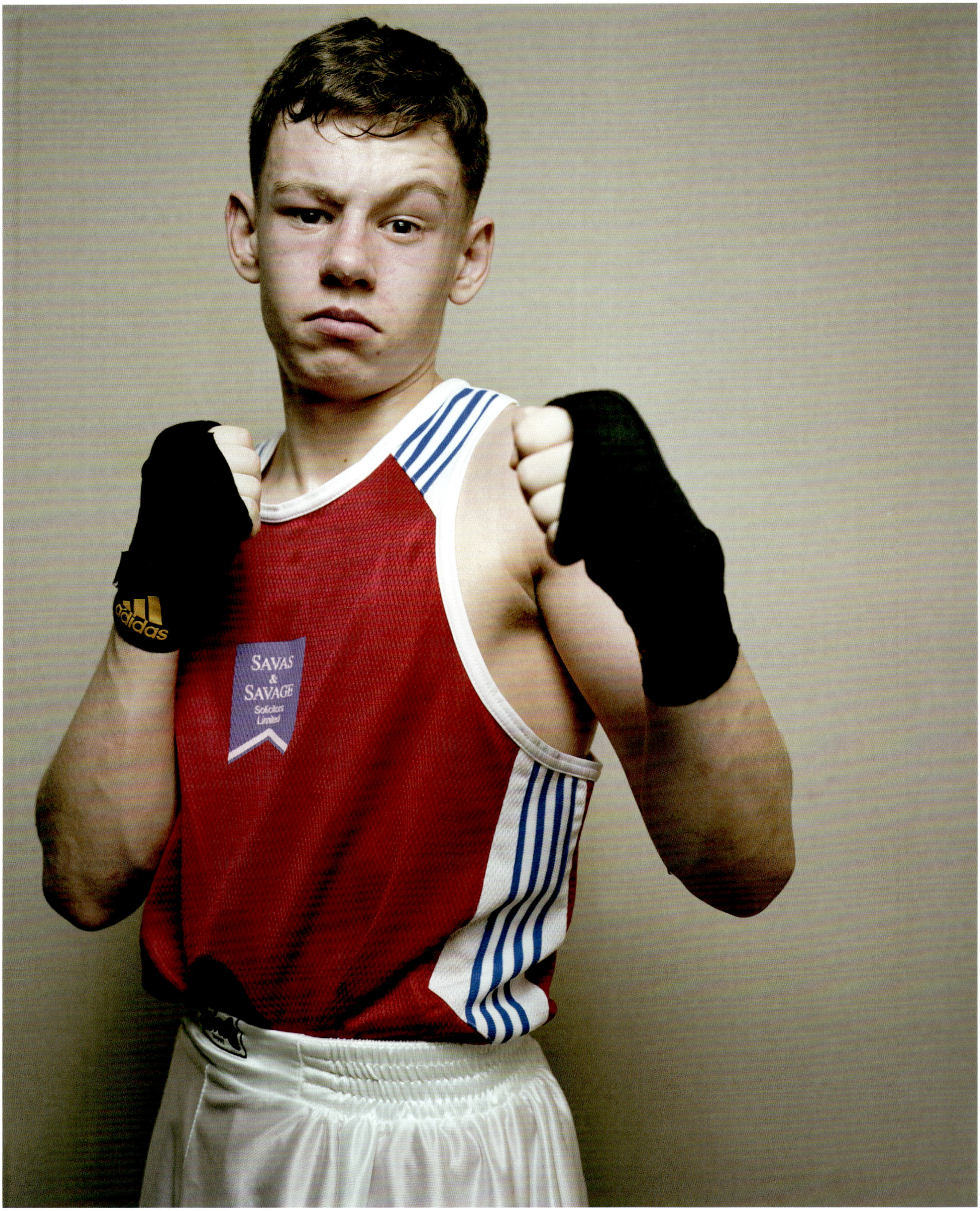
adidas
SAVAS
&
SAVAGE
Solicitors
Limited

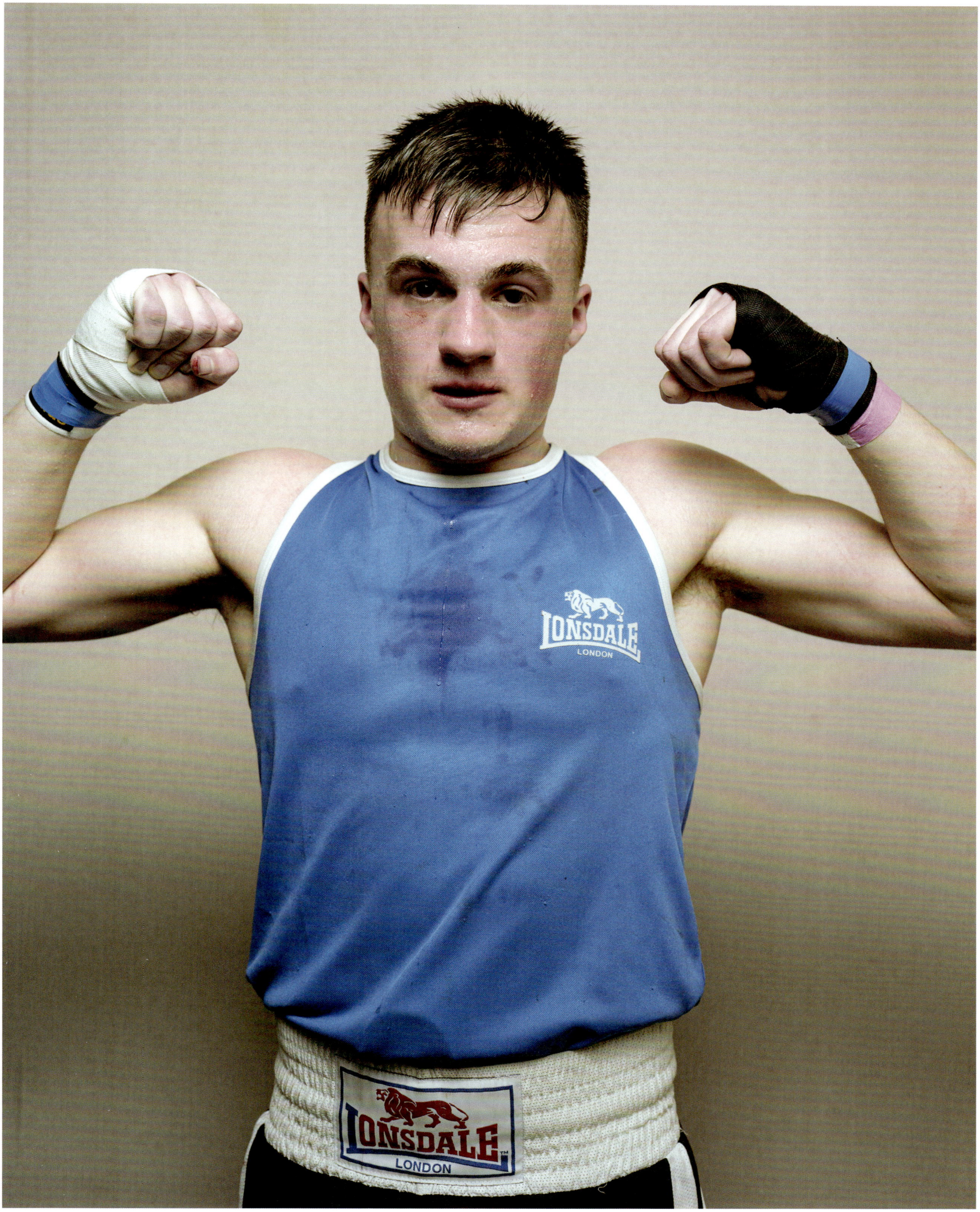
LONSDALE
LONDON
LONSDALE
LONDON

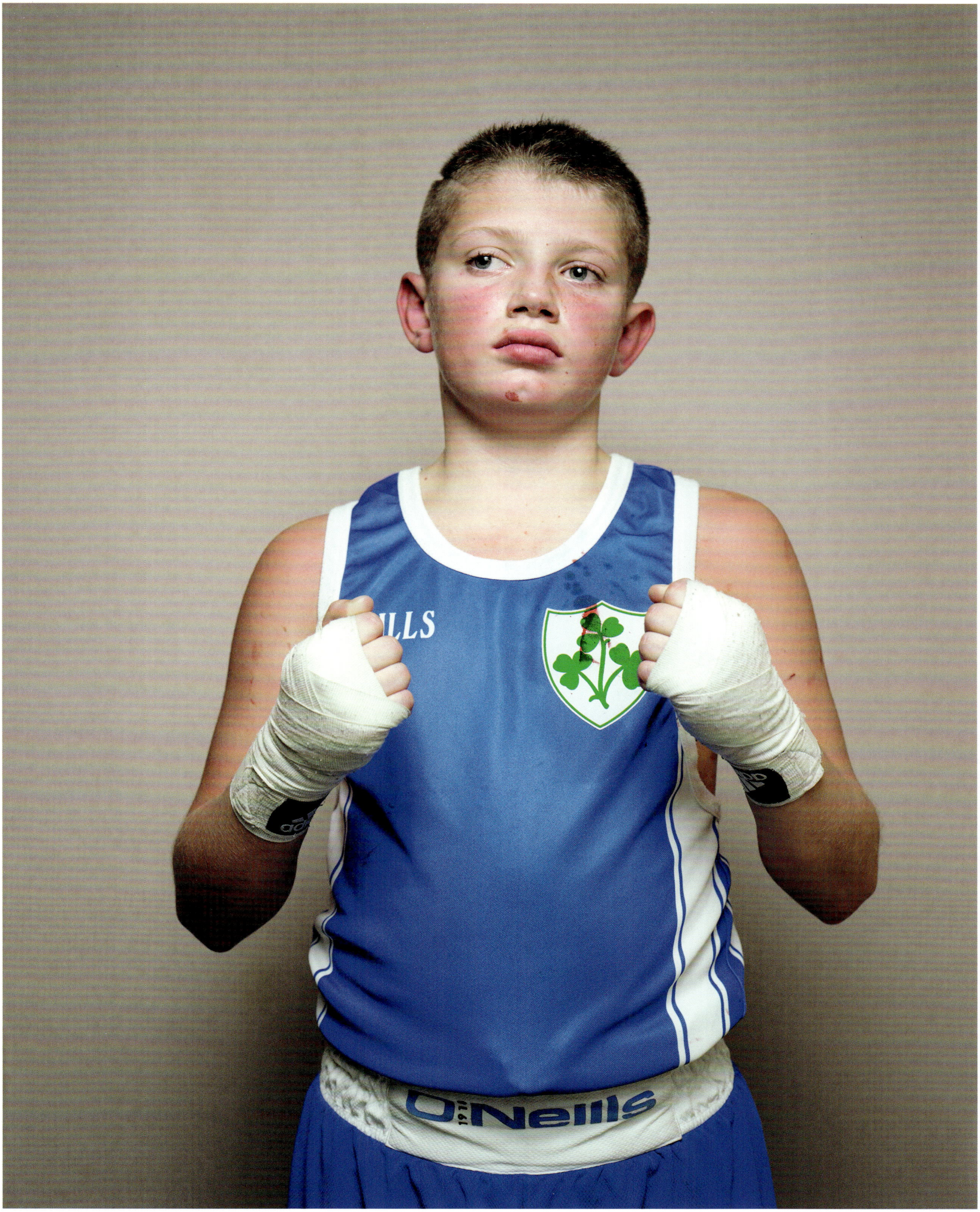
O'Neills

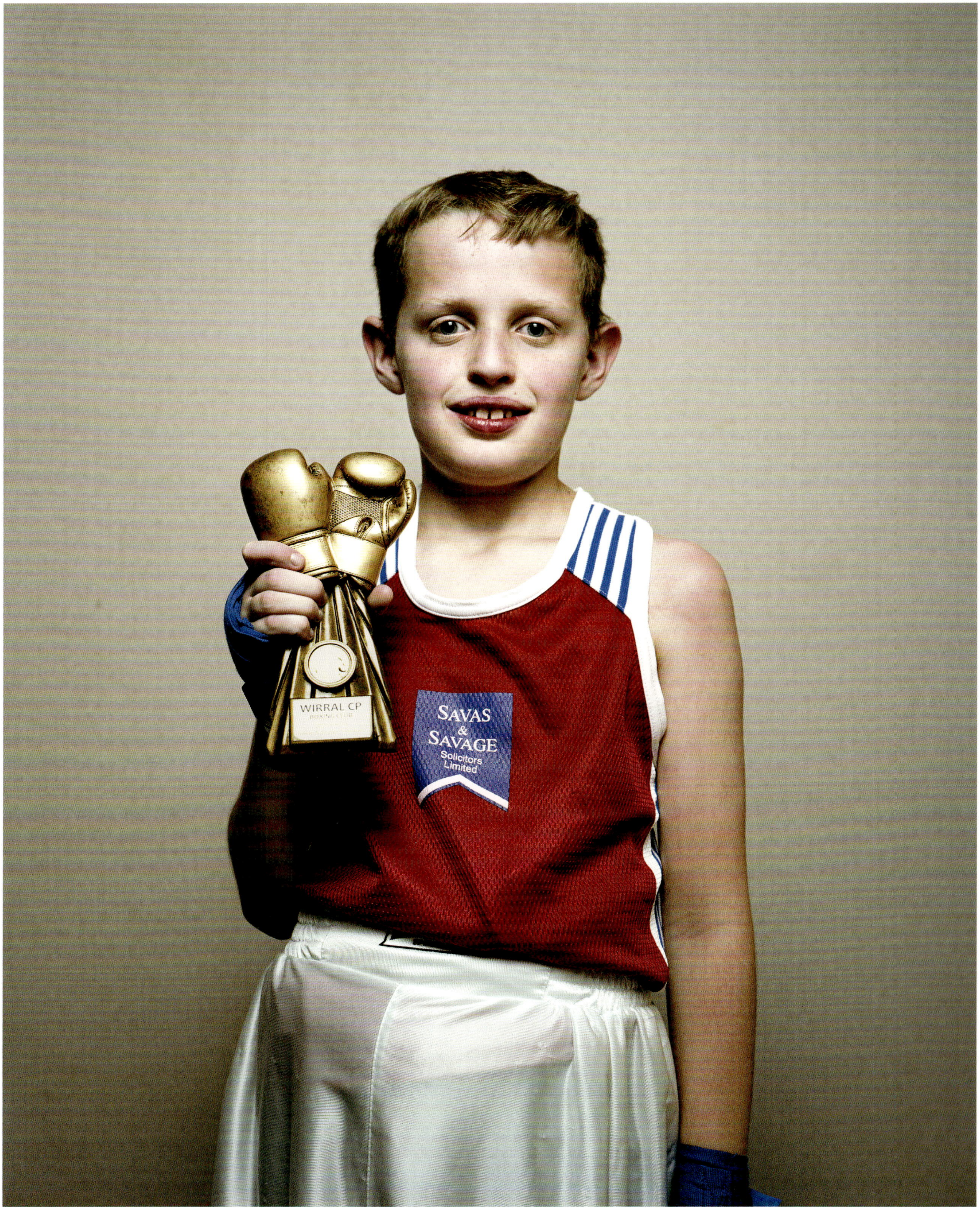
WIRRAL CP
SAVAS & SAVAGE
Solicitors Limited

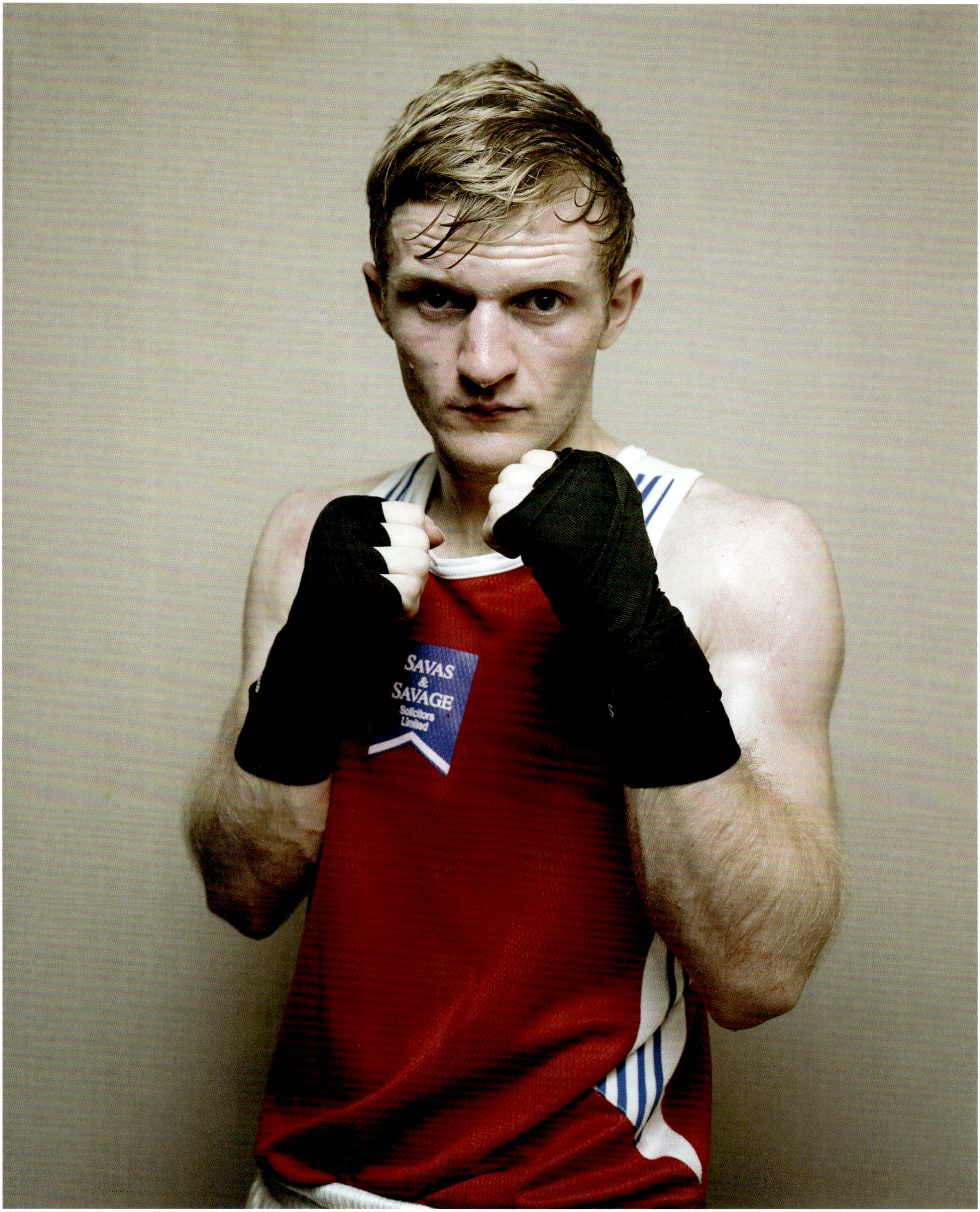
SAVAS
&
SAVAGE
Solicitors
Limited

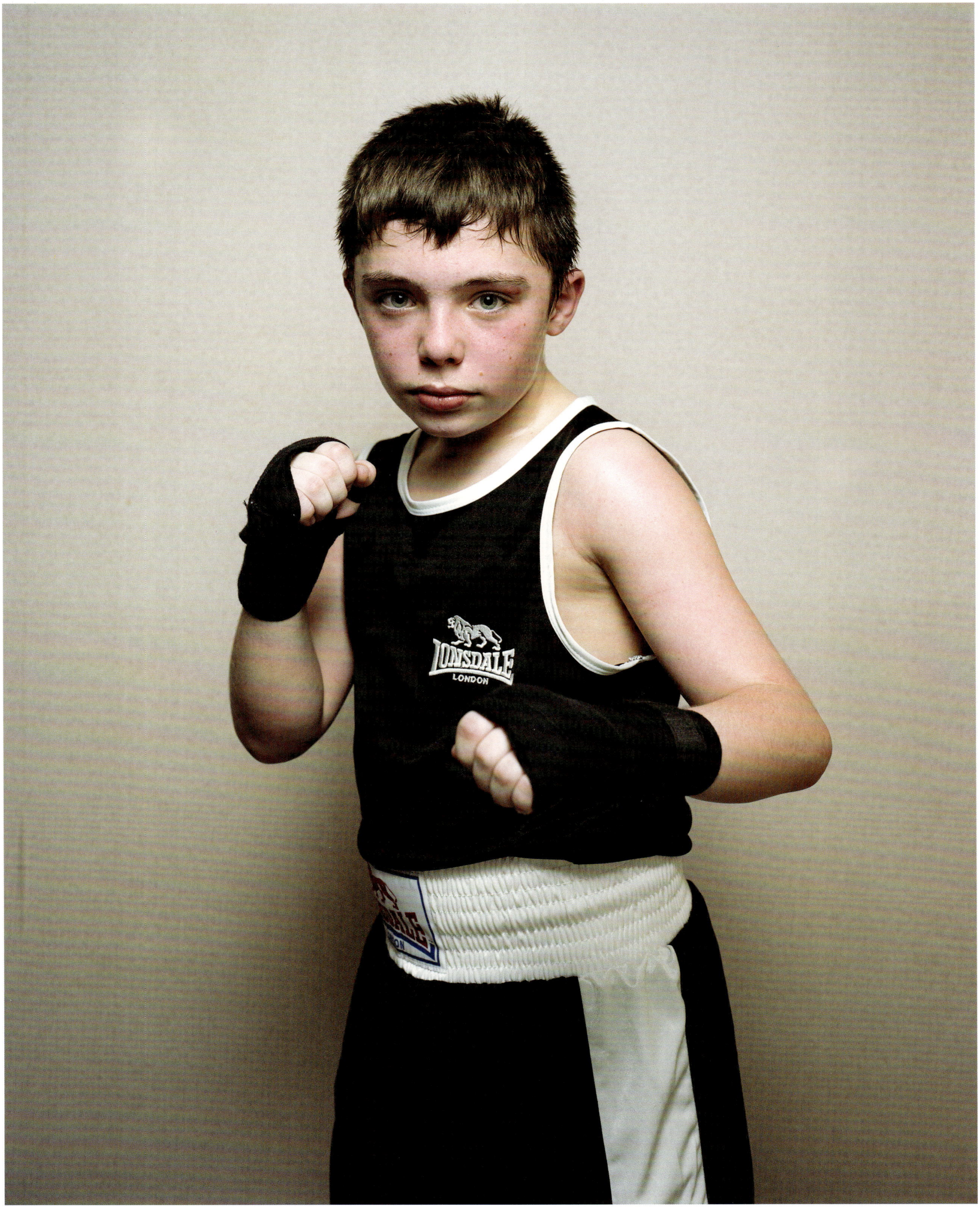
LONSDALE
LONDON

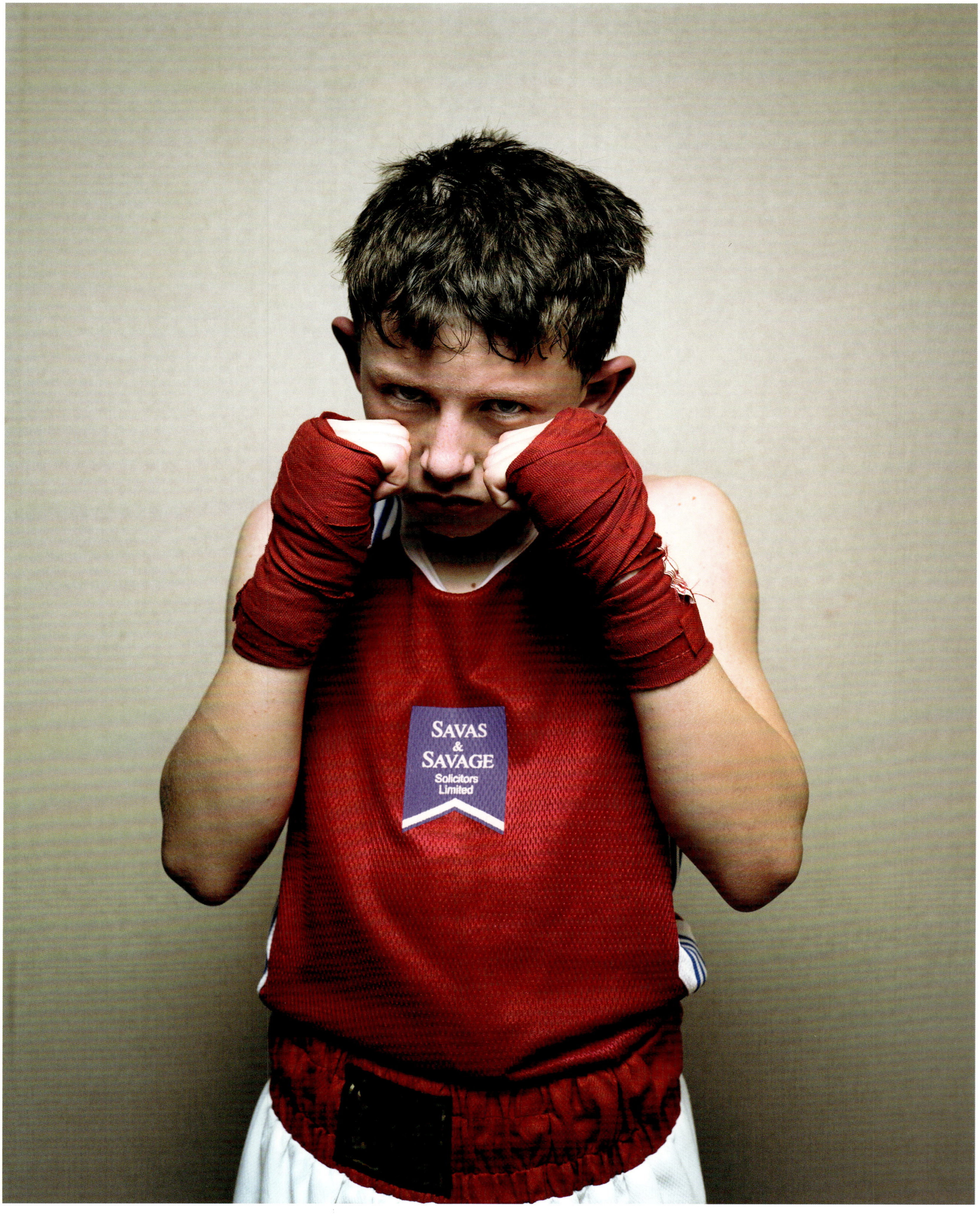
SAVAS
&
SAVAGE
Solicitors
Limited

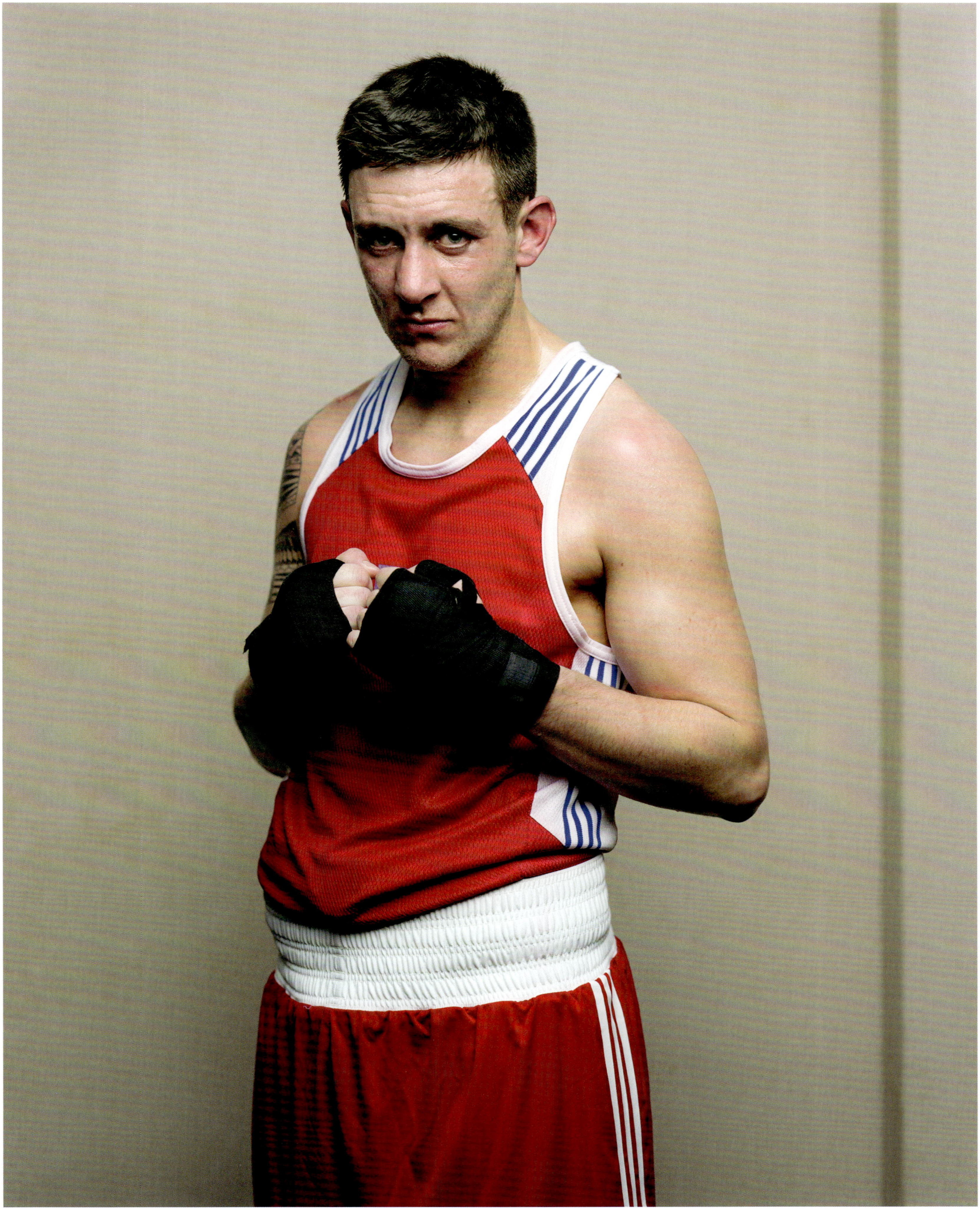

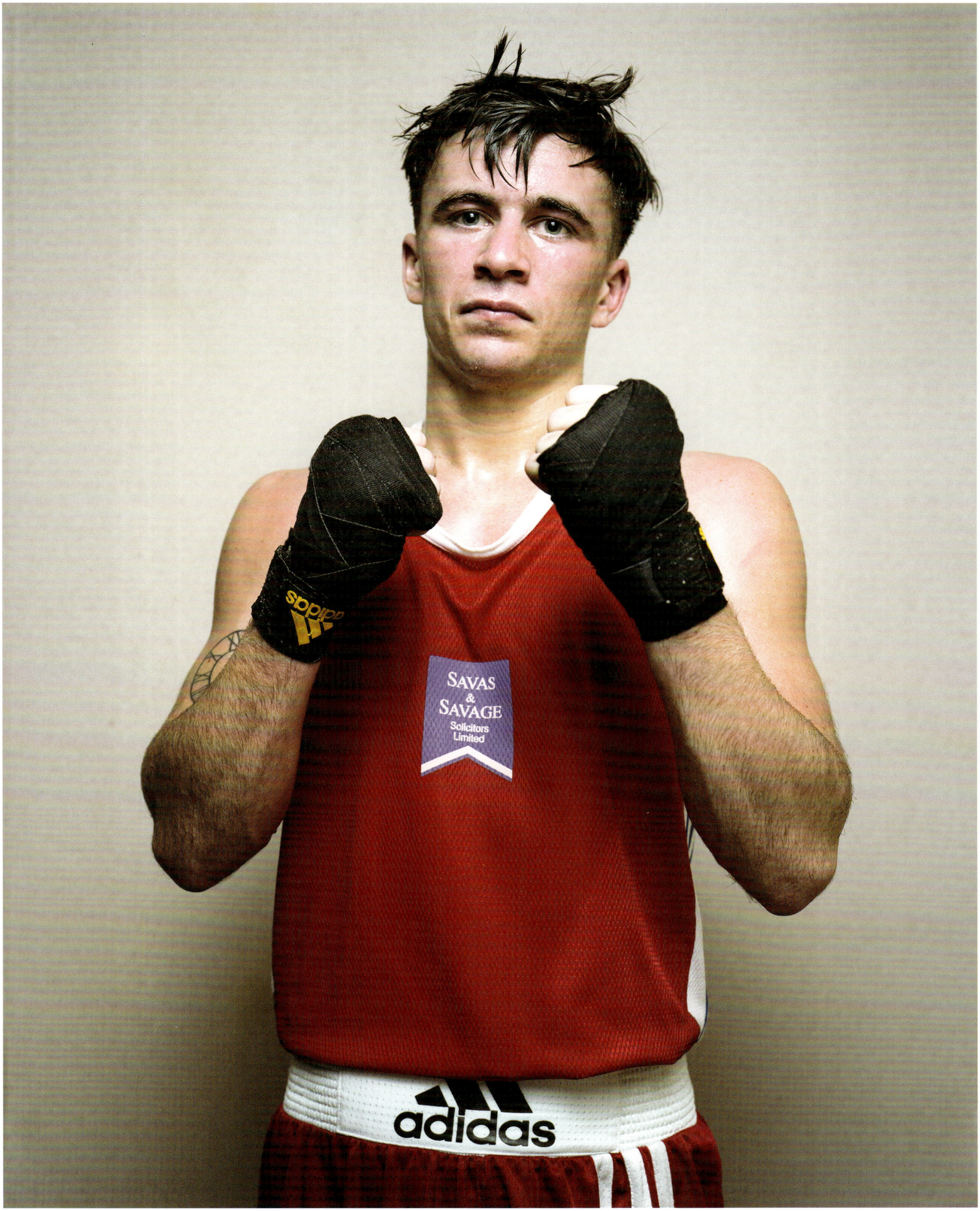
adidas
SAVAS
&
SAVAGE
Solicitors
Limited
adidas

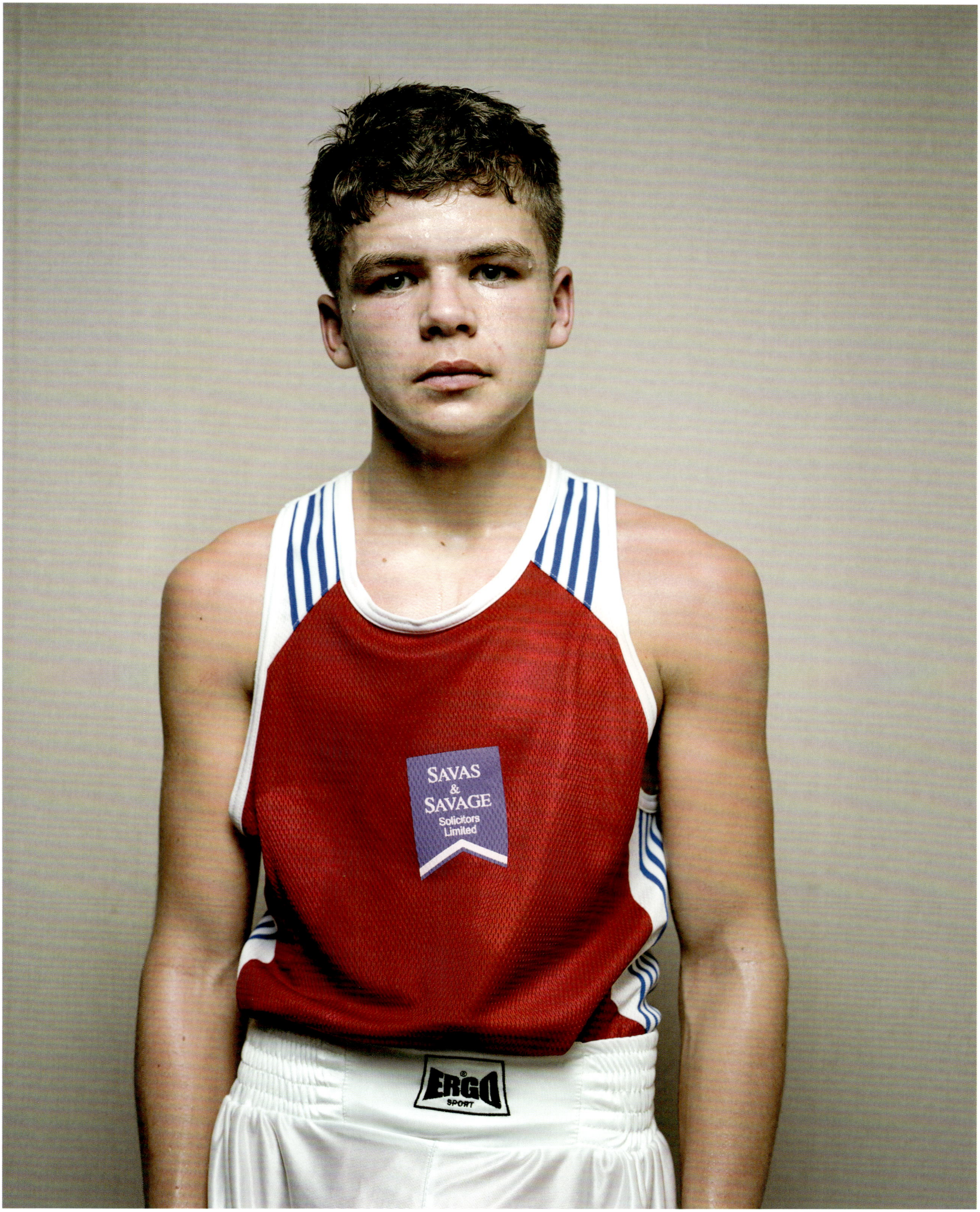
SAVAS
&
SAVAGE
Solicitors
Limited
ERGO
SPORT

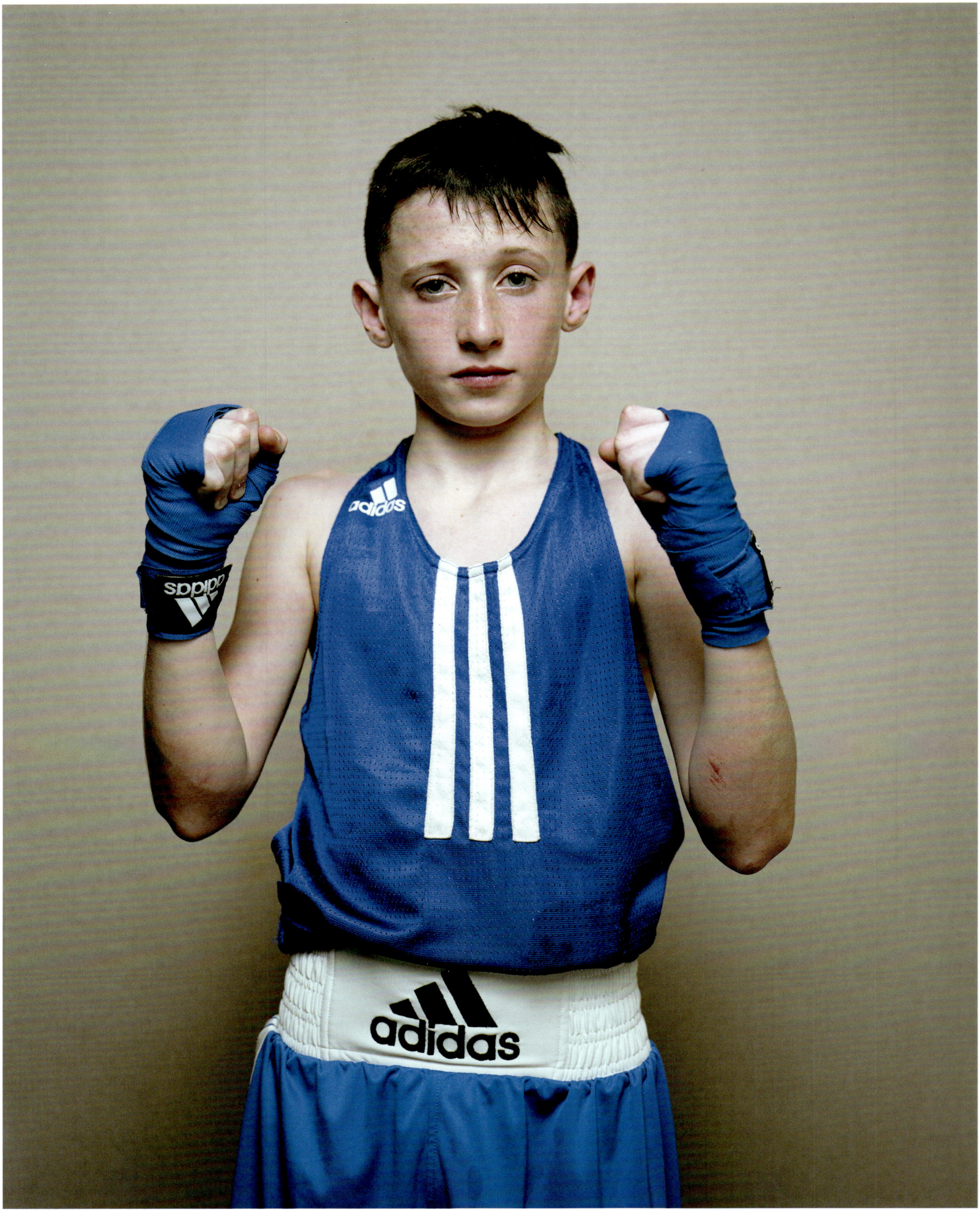
adidas
adidas

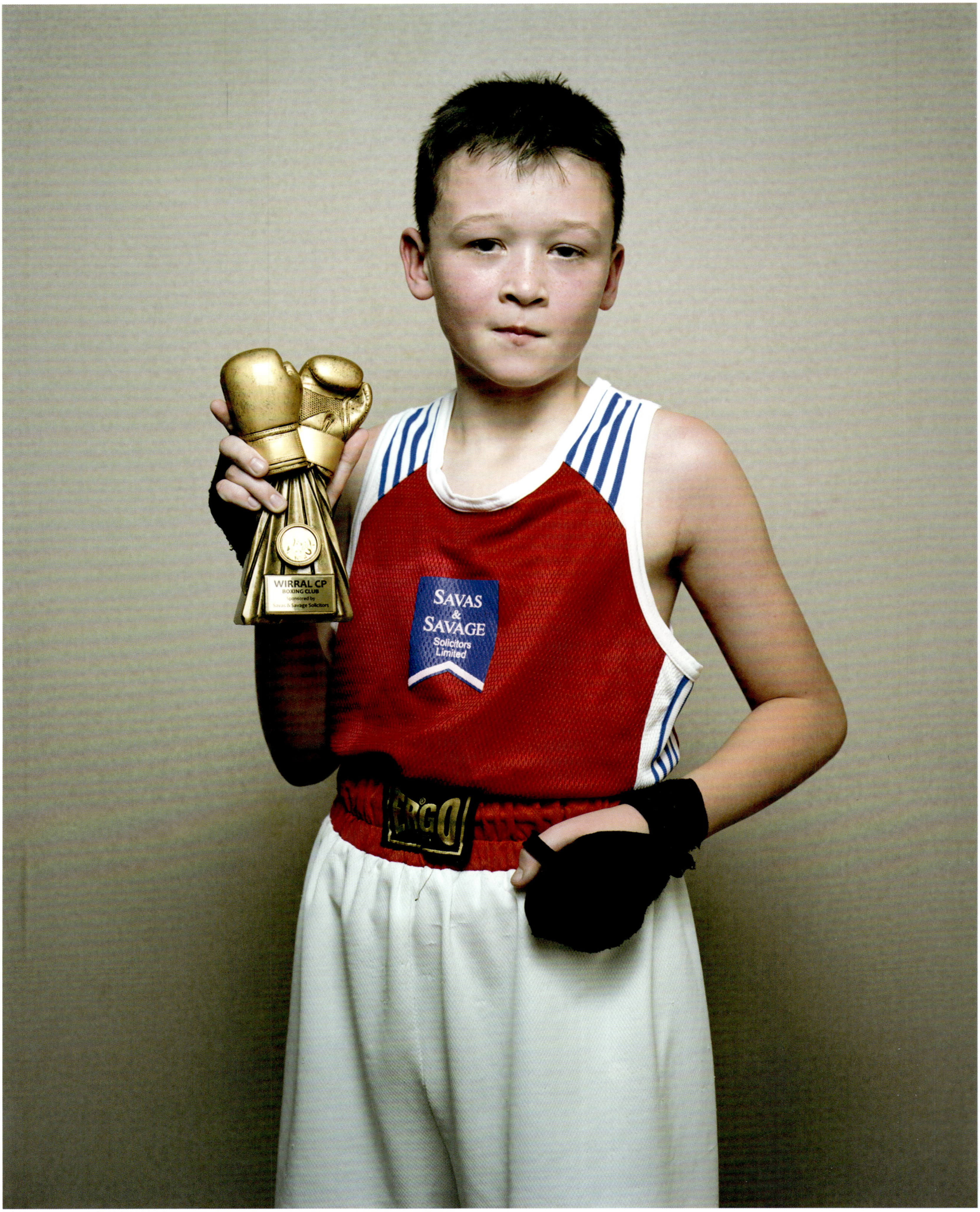
WIRRAL CP
BOXING CLUB
SAVAS
&
SAVAGE
Solicitors
Limited
ERGO

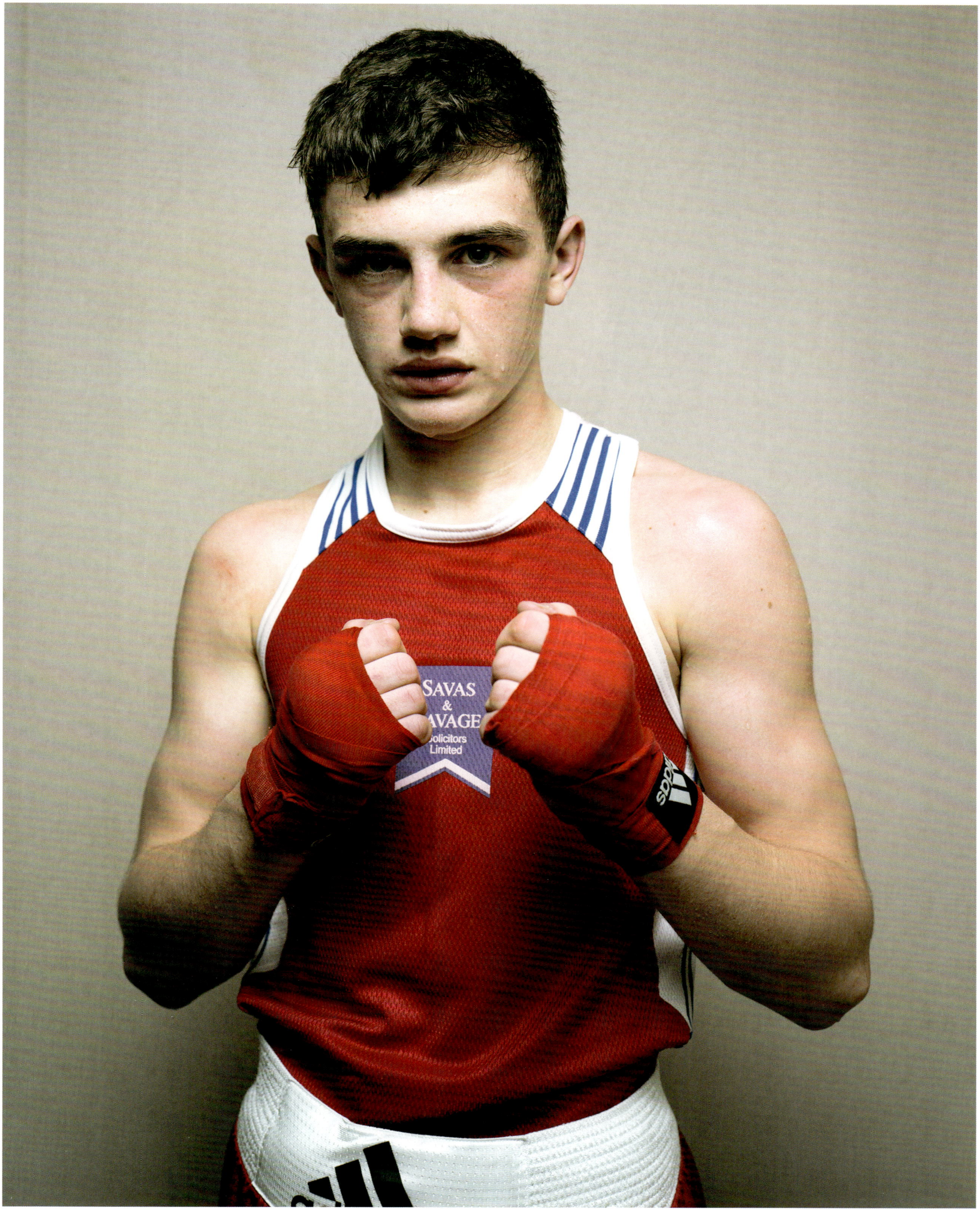
SAVAS
&
AVAGE
Solicitors
Limited

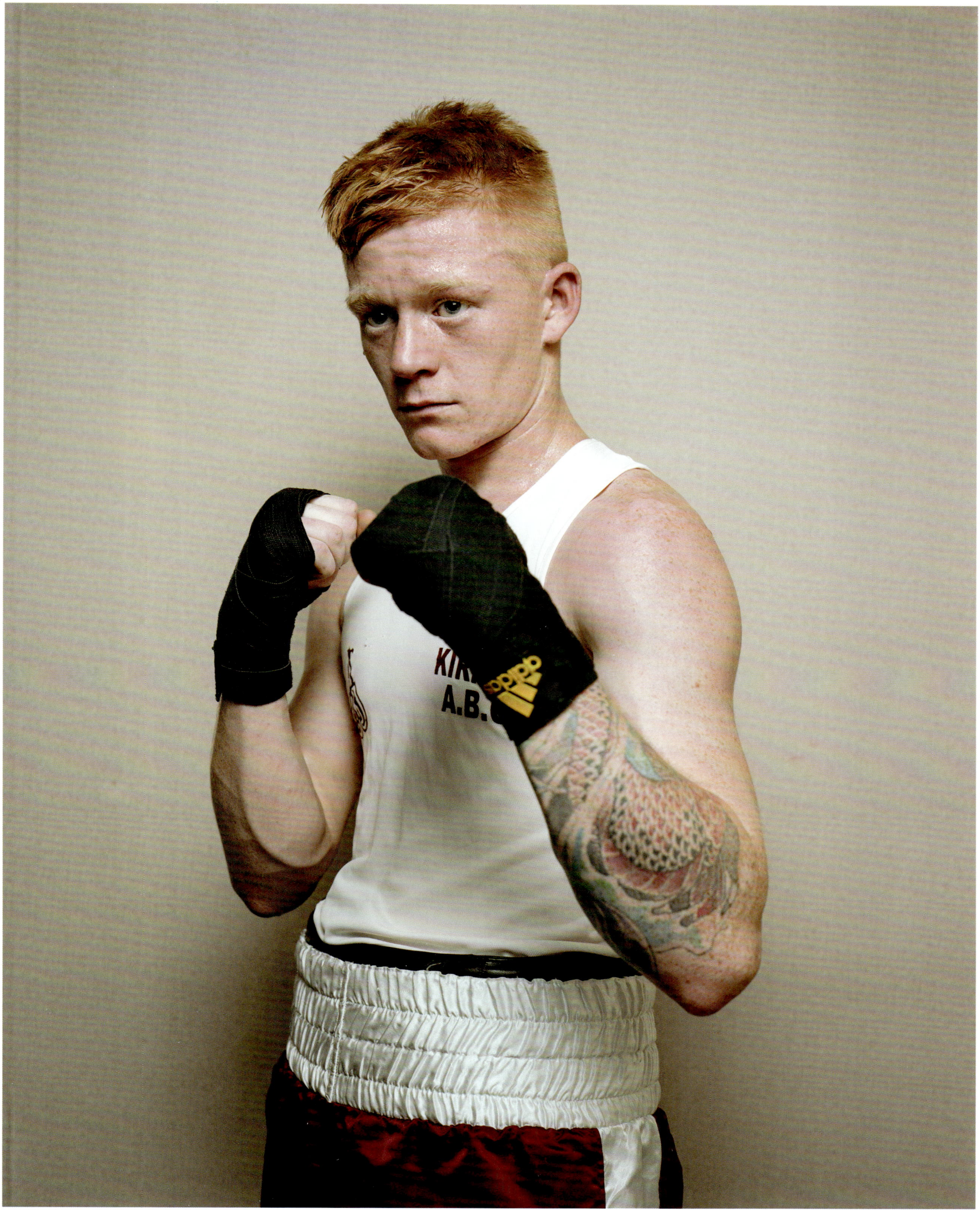
adidas

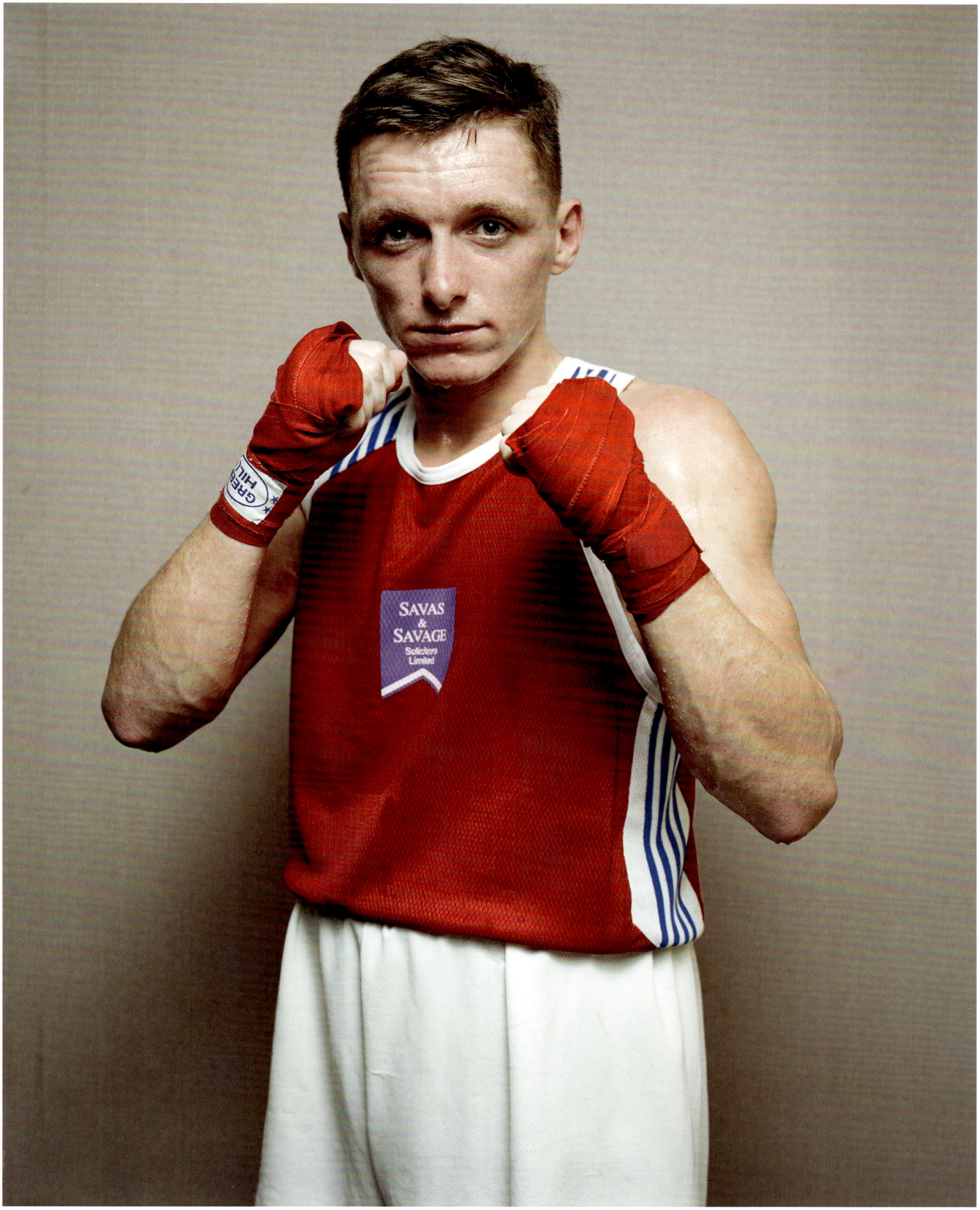
SAVAS
&
SAVAGE
Solicitors
Limited

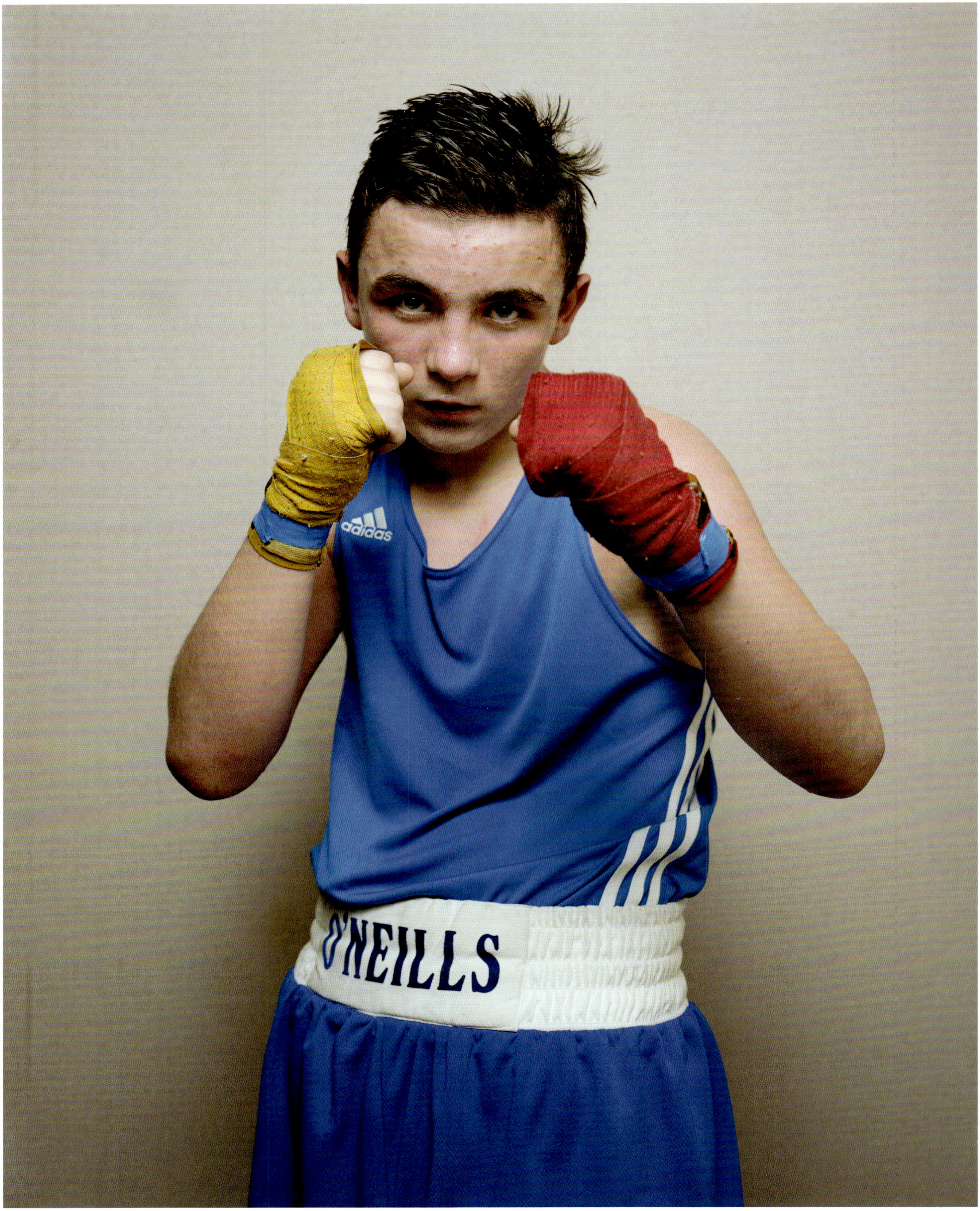
adidas
O'NEILLS

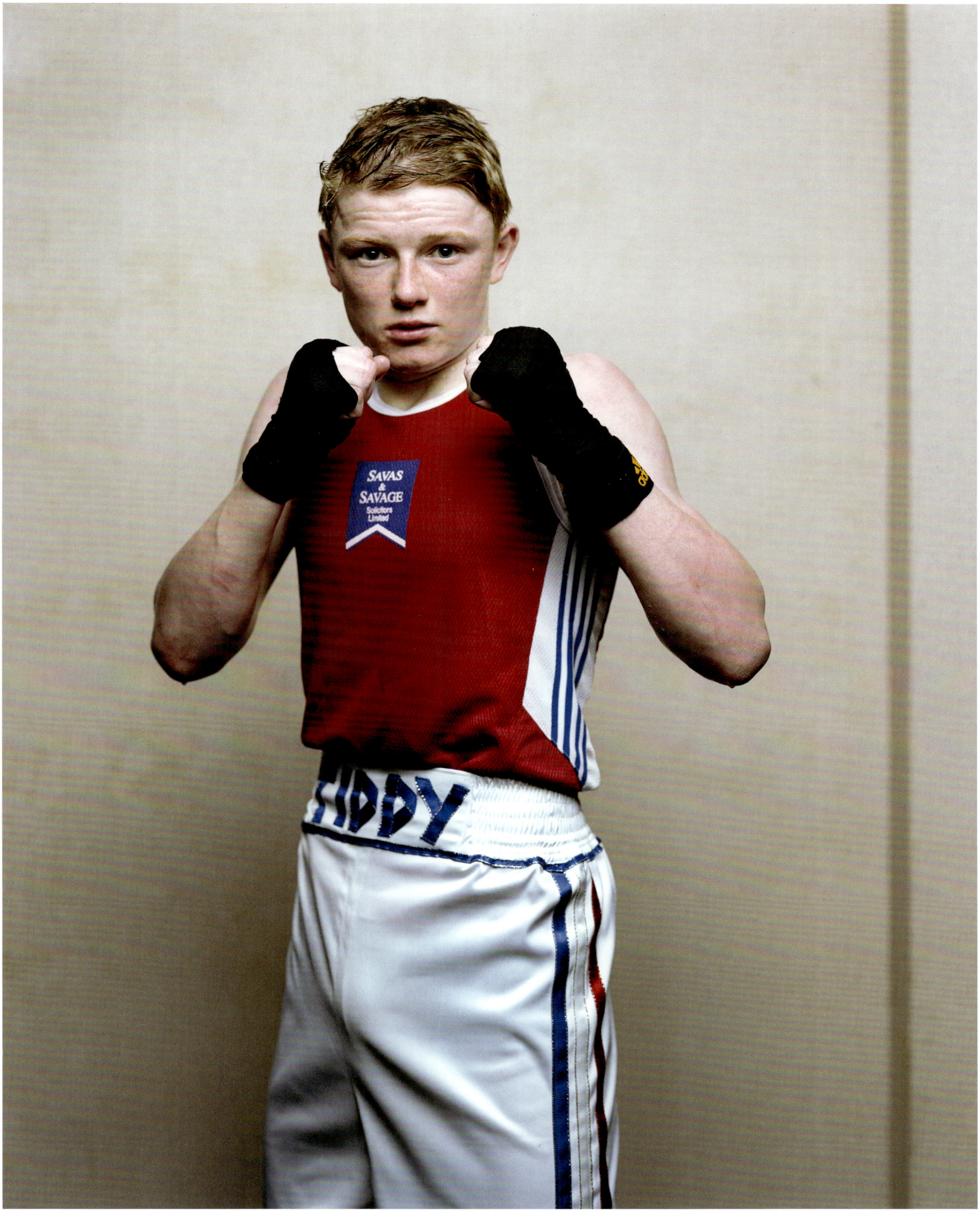
SAVAS & SAVAGE
Solicitors Limited

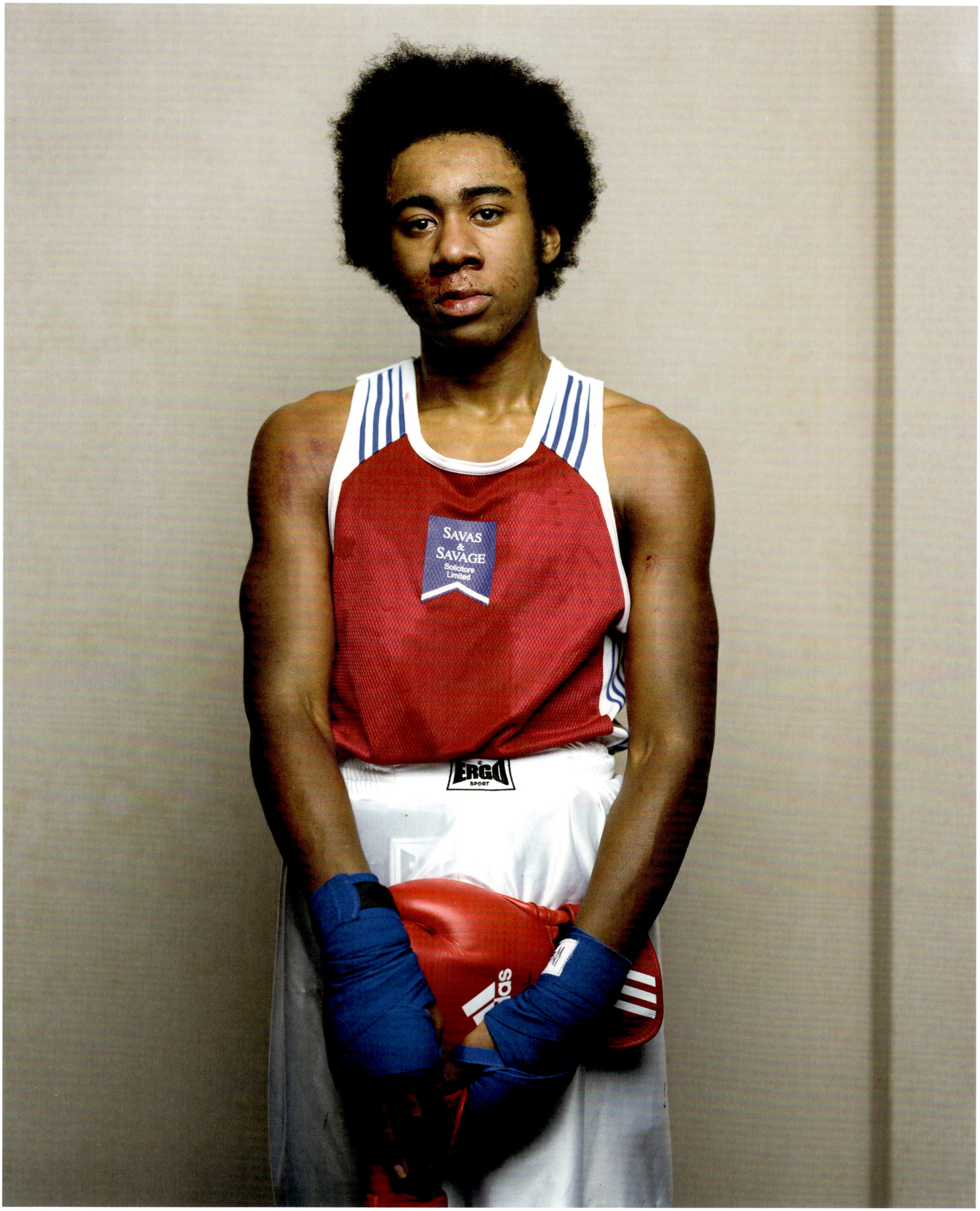
SAVAS & SAVAGE
Solicitors Limited
ERGO
SPORT

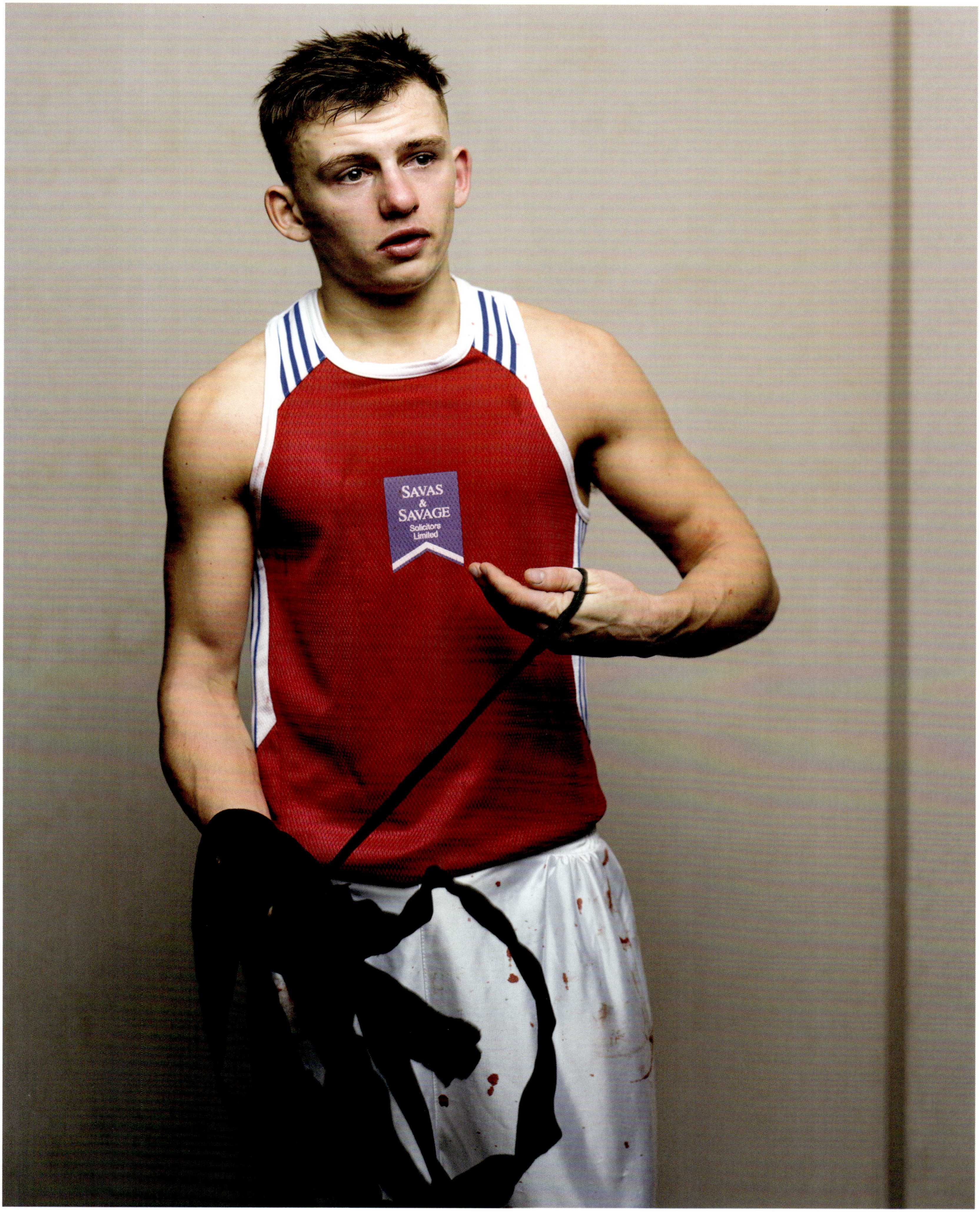
SAVAS & SAVAGE
Solicitors Limited

…I can entertain the proposition that life is a metaphor for boxing — for one of those bouts that go on and on, round following round, jabs, missed punches, clinches, nothing determined, again the bell and again and you and your opponent so evenly matched it's impossible not to see that your opponent *is* you…

Joyce Carol Oates,
On Boxing

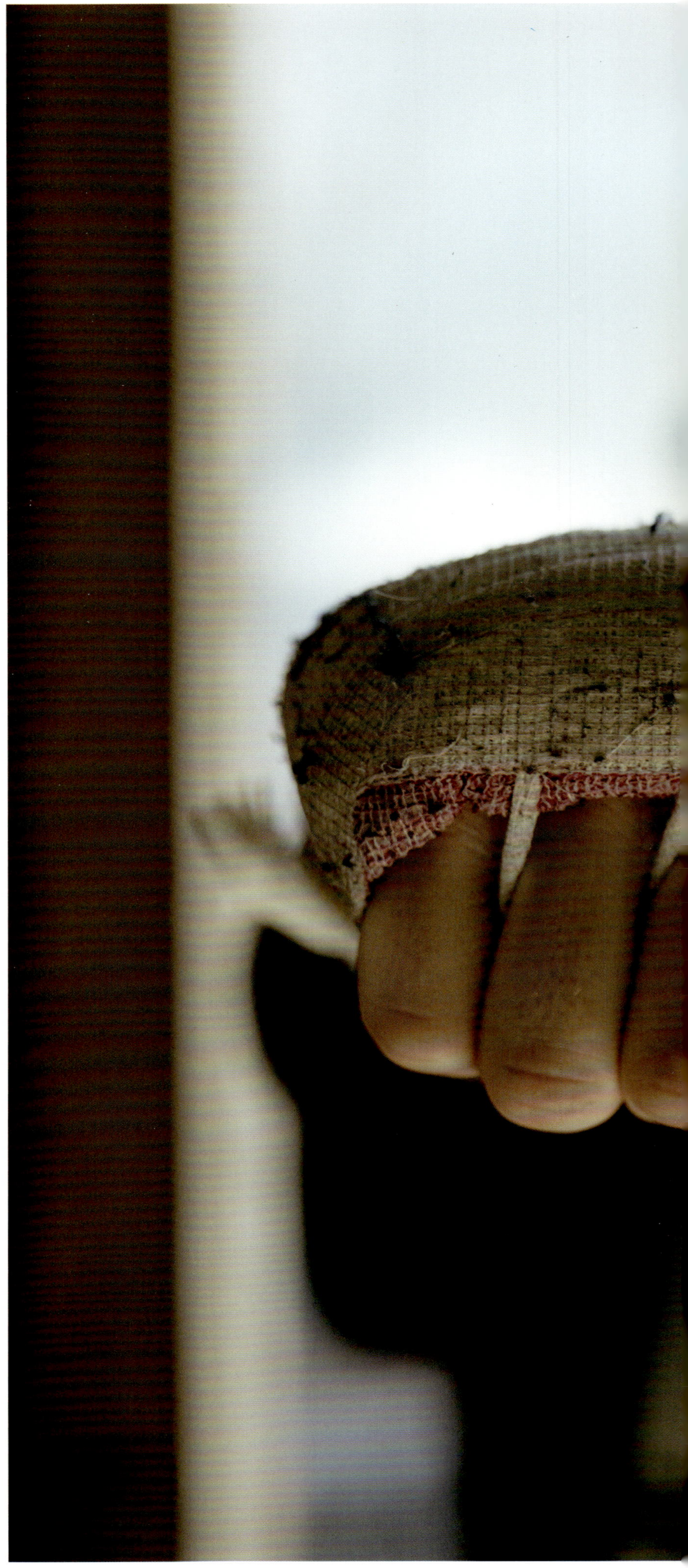

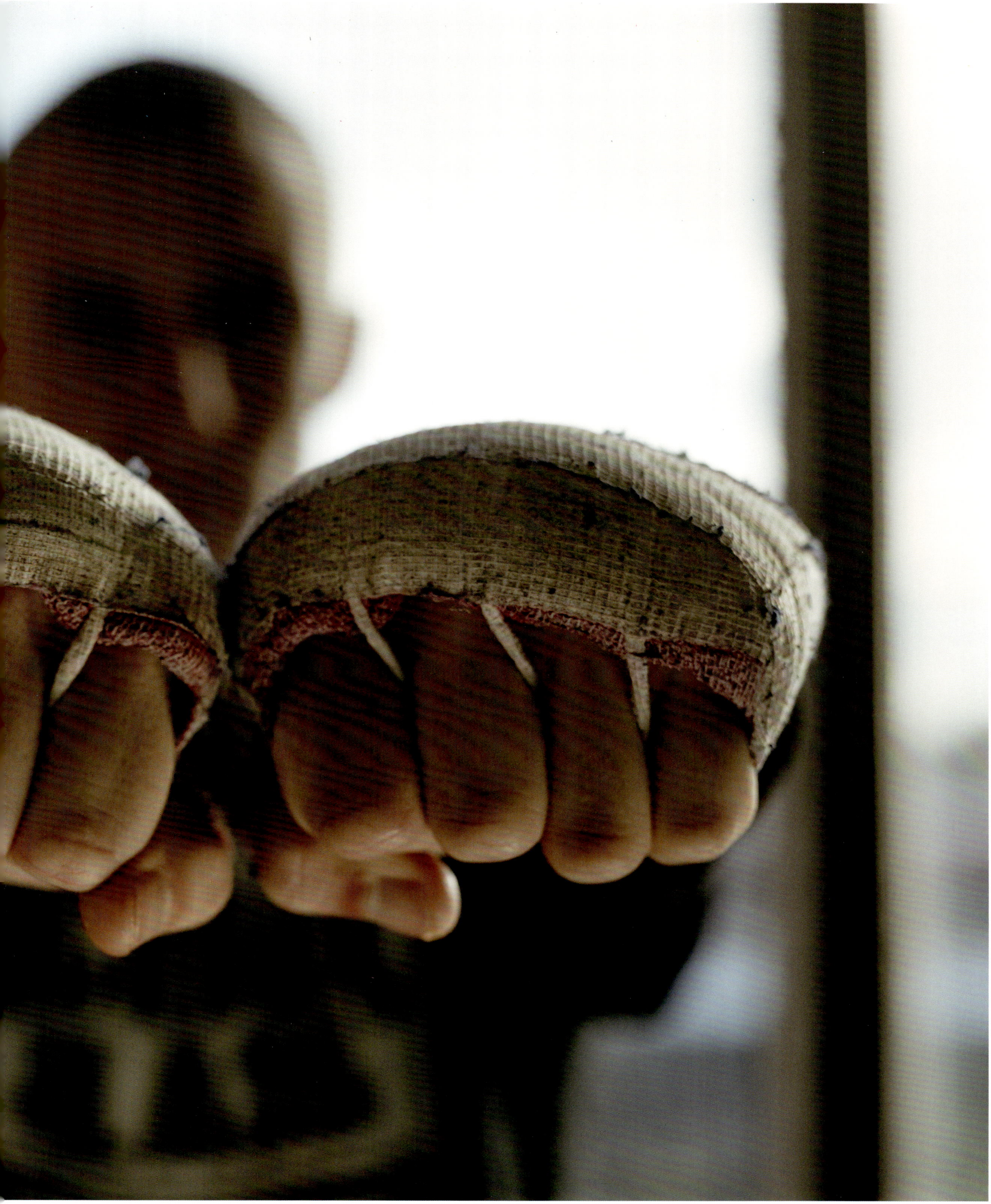

IMAGES

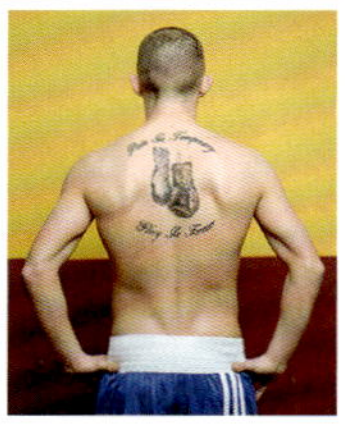

The Champ

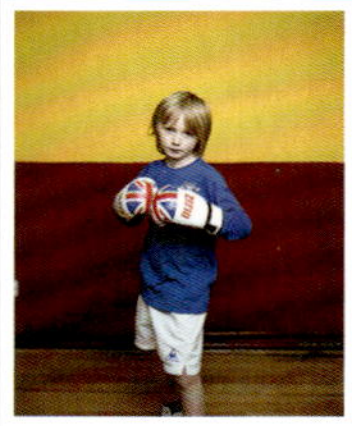

Kenzie.
Training

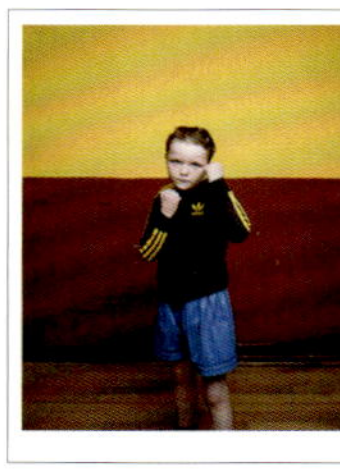

Peter.
Training

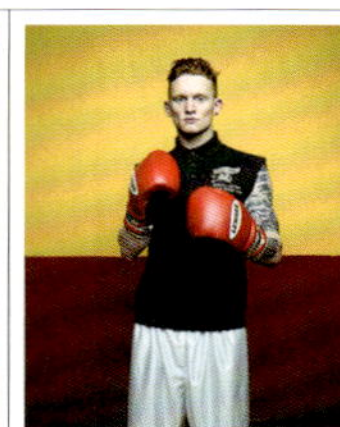

Mason.
Training

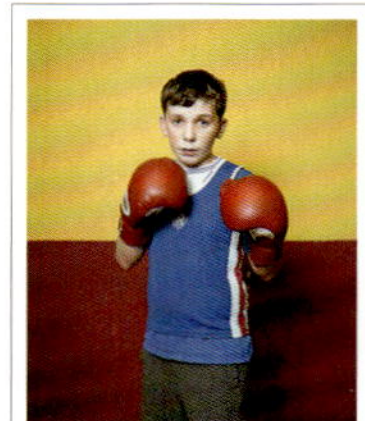

Tony.
Training

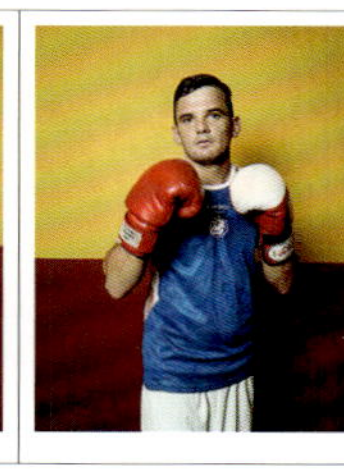

Alex.
Training

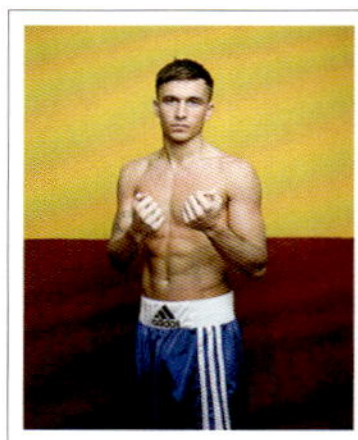

Jamie K.
Training

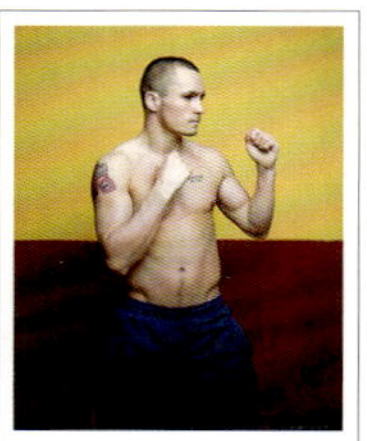

Matty.
Training

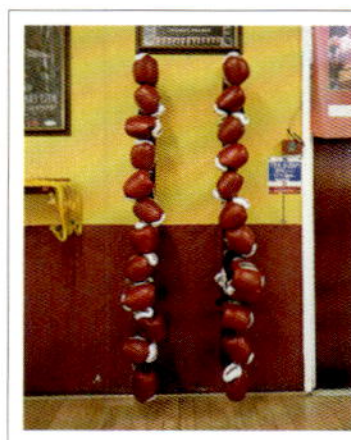

Training #1.
Wirral Club

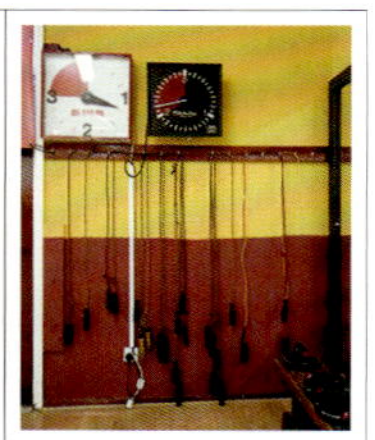

Training #2.
Wirral Club

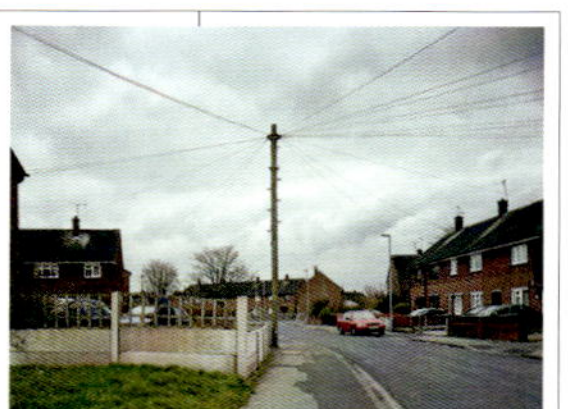

The Port #1

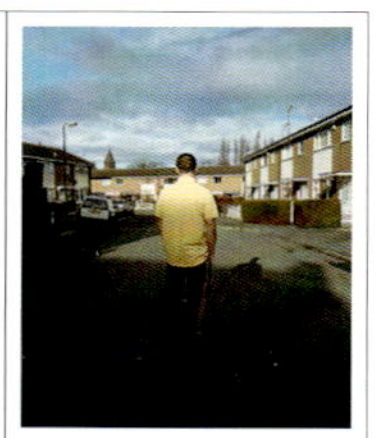

The Port #2

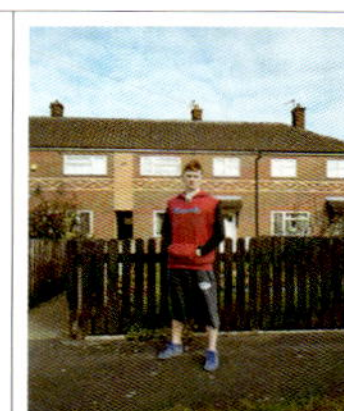

Mason.
Neighborhood

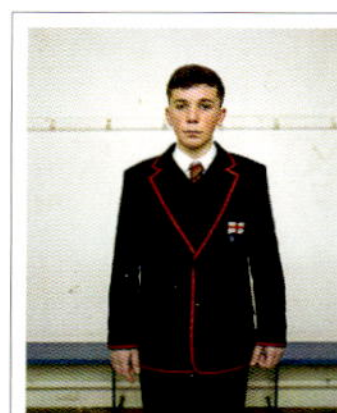

Tony.
School Uniform

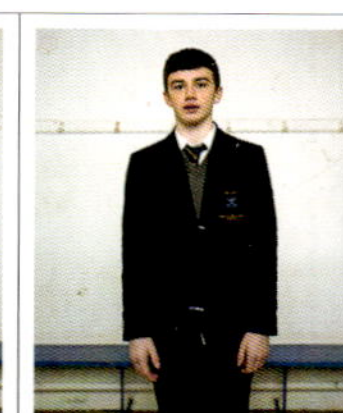

Kyle.
School Uniform

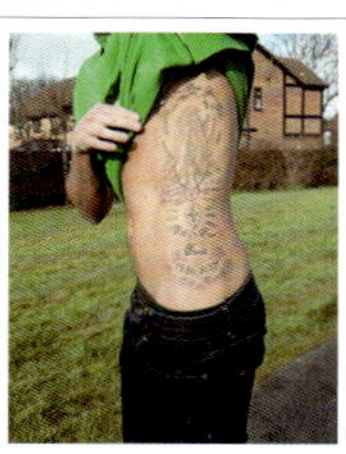

Alex.
Tattoo for Daniel

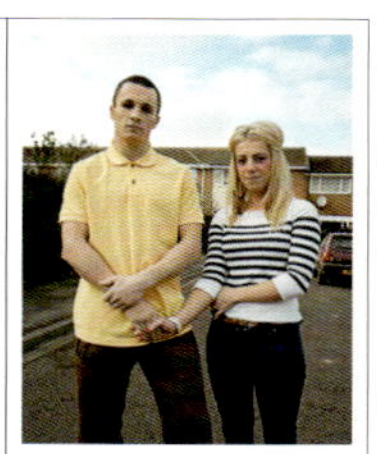

Matty and
Chelsea

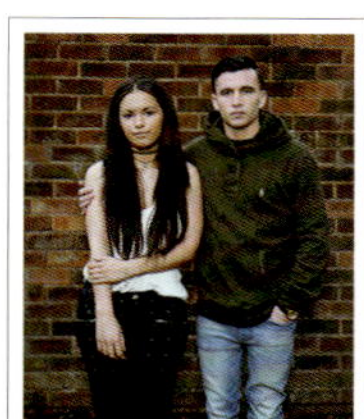

Jamie K. and
Beth

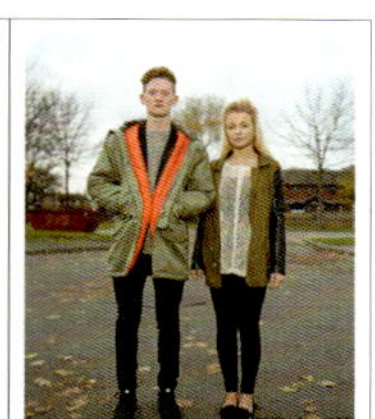

Mason and
Chelsea

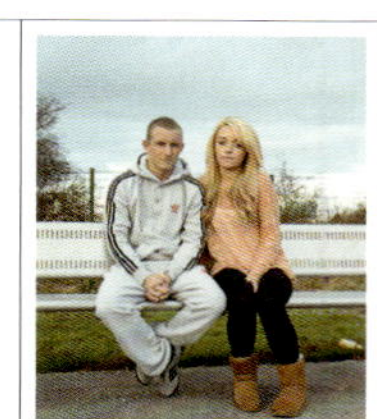

Paul and
Sadie

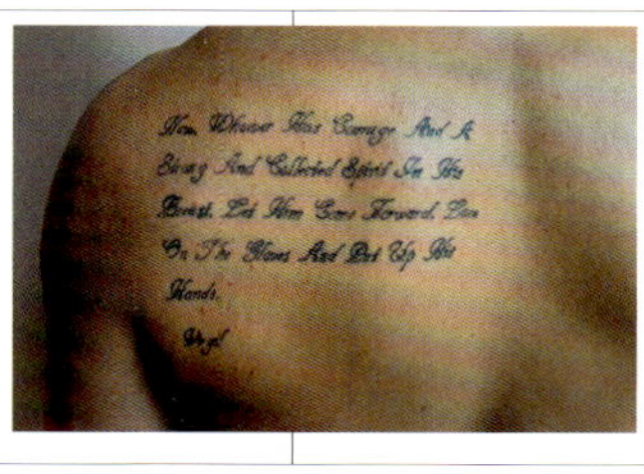

Carl's Back

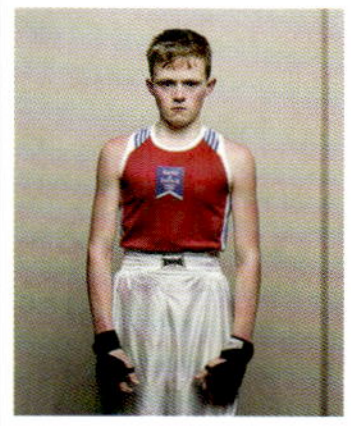

James.
Wirral Club

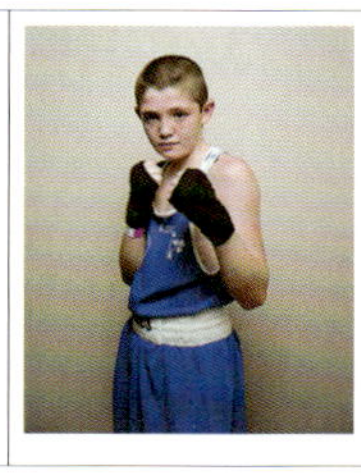

Ben.
Crumlin Club

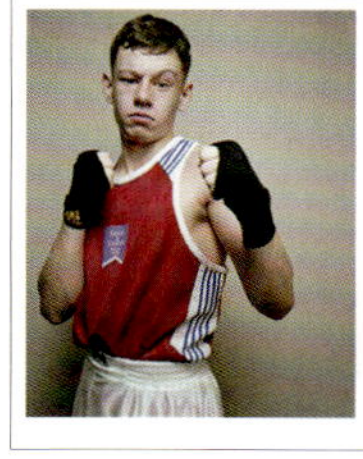

Josh.
Wirral Club

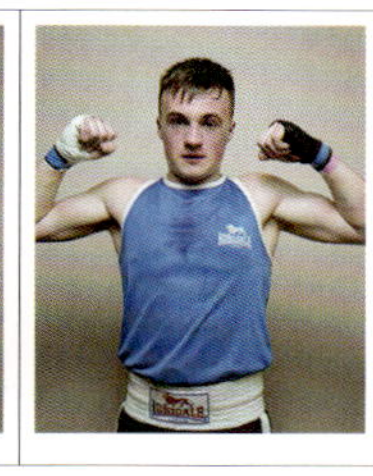

Luke.
Crumlin Club

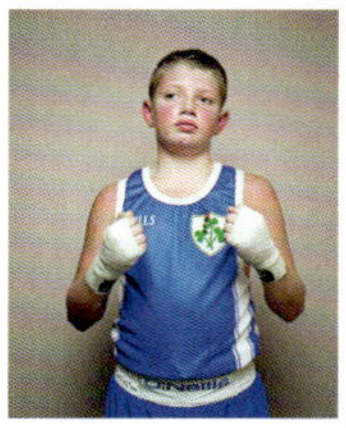

William.
Crumlin Club

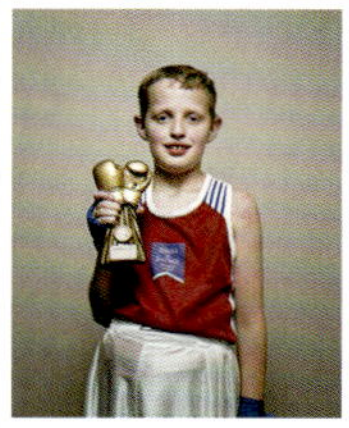

Jamie S.
Wirral Club

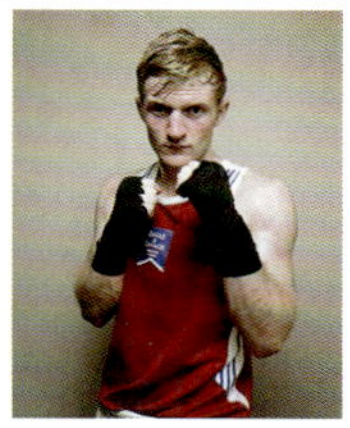

Will.
Wirral Club

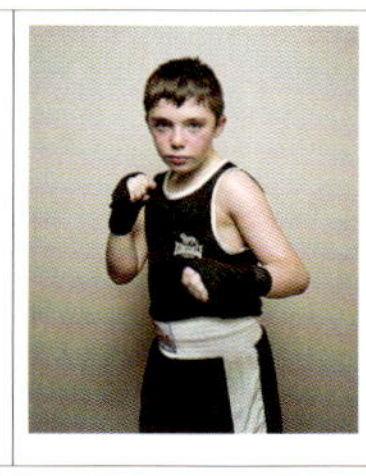

Noeley.
Wirral Club

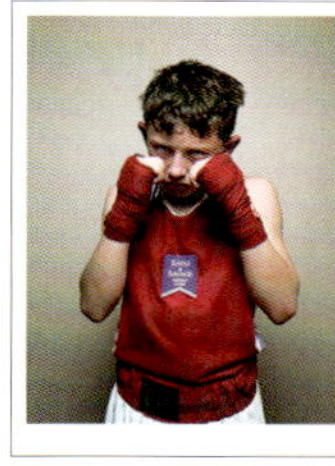

Jack M.
Wirral Club

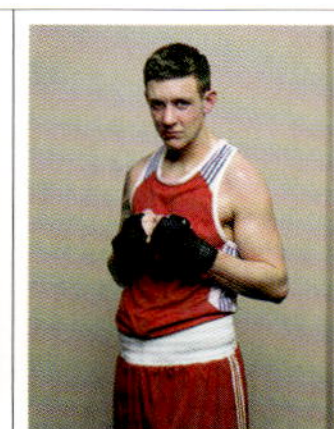

Carl.
Wirral Club

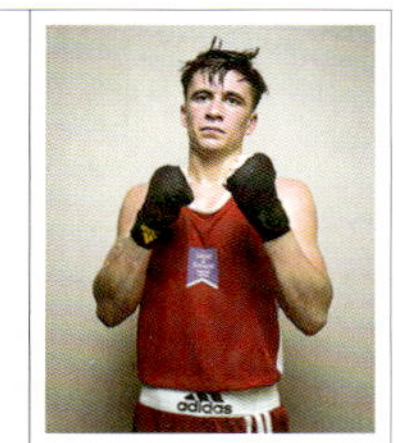

Jamie K.
Wirral Club

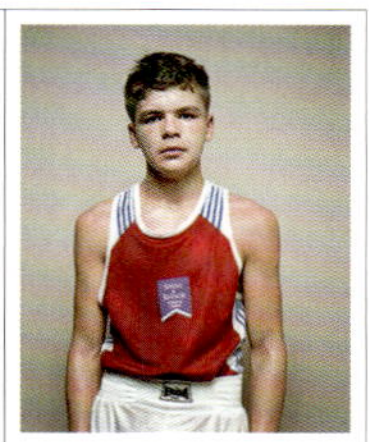

Connor.
Wirral Club

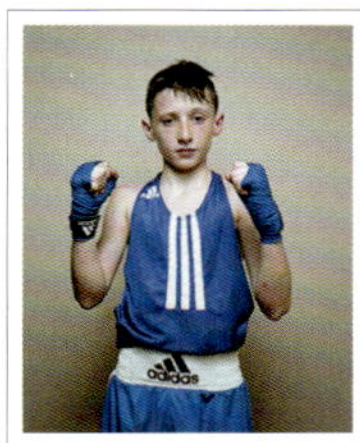

Keane.
Crumlin Club

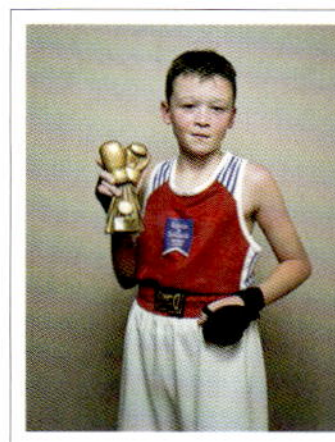

Brad.
Wirral Club

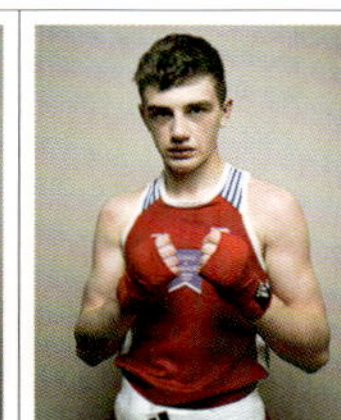

Kyle.
Wirral Club

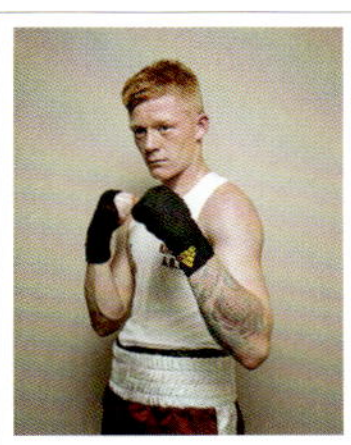

Jake.
Kirby Club

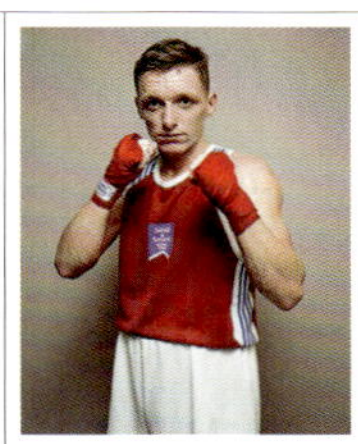

Alfie.
Wirral Club

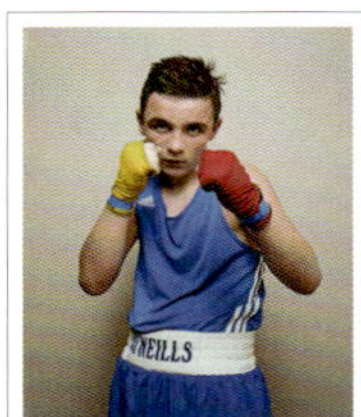

Glen.
Crumlin Club

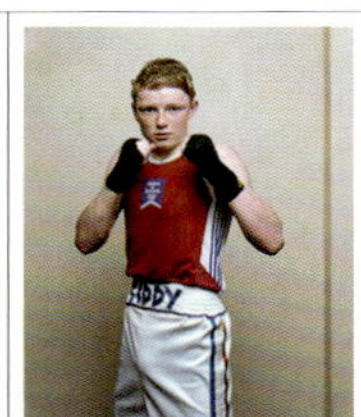

Tiddy.
Wirral Club

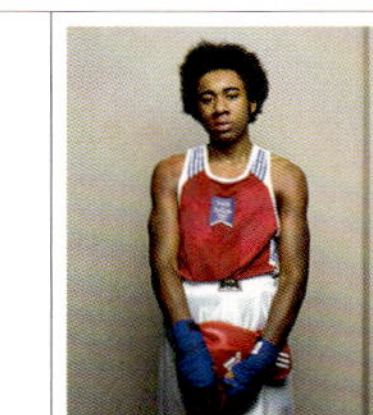

Marlon.
Wirral Club

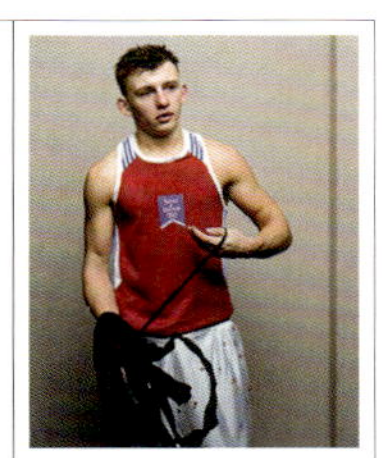

Jack K.
Wirral Club

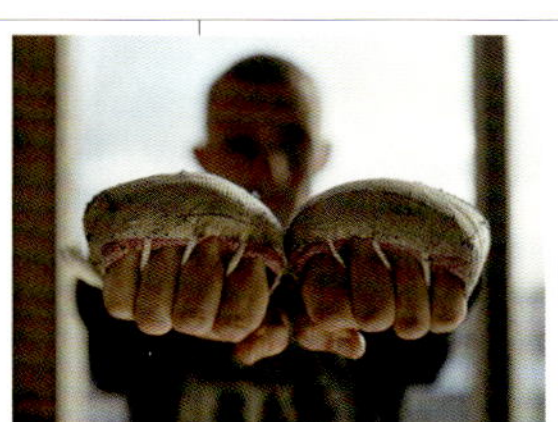

The Champ #2

THANK YOU

For connecting the words and pictures:
Bruce Weber, Nan Bush, Laura Dern

Production Fixer – Team Lawson:
Steve, Tracy and Sophie

Editorial Advisor:
Alan Rapp

Production Assistance:
Jason Tlush Studio
Tony Window / Metro Lab
Erik Auerbach, Heidi Yount, Tom Phillipson, Andrew Sloat

Lost Planet:
Chris Kursel, Hank Corwin, Gary Ward

Travel Coordination:
Geoff Evans

For help, assistance, advice and direction:
Mary Trunk, Andrew Turman, Jaclyn Paris, Brett Mayfield, Matt Berardi, Hillery Estes, Craig Barron, Radha Hall, Alberto Orso, Jeff Lee, Holly Goldberg Sloan, K.C. Elliott, Dorothee Mitrani, Taqi Kizilbash, Marcela Widrig, Jen Chaiken, Julie Silliman, Alison Van Pelt

Shelley Desoto, David Maisel, Judy Keller, Lindsay Morris, Julian Cox, Colin Westerbeck, Jori Finkel, Elizabeth Smith, Alicia Miller

Rose and Robert Frank, Lorna Loungway

Home Team:
Kent Tsurumaru

The Mom Squad:
Tara Amiel, Susannah Grant, Loren Montgomery, Moye Thompson, Alex Rockwell

For welcoming me and sharing your stories:

Team Butler:
Paul Butler Jr., Paul Butler Sr., Gill Butler, Anthony Farnell, Sadie Jones

Wirral Community Boxing Club:
Peter "Macca" Phelan, Lee Holmes, John Kennedy

Alex Foulkes, Kenzie Moore, Tony Moore, Peter McCann, Mason Cartwright, Matty Fagan Kyle Timson, James Delaney, Josh Quinn, Jack McEvoy, Marlon Walters, Sean Griffiths, Tom Jellicoe, Will Fewtrell, Reece Goodhall, Jamie Summerfield, Jack McLeod, Carl McLeod, Connor Leatt, Eddie Thompson, Bradley Powell, Morgan Handley, Jack Tidd, Jamie and Jack Kelly, Elliott James, Chelsea Pritchard, Bethany Richmond, Chelsea Millward

Crumlin Club, Dublin:
Philip Sutcliffe

Luke Boyle, Keane Doyle, Glen Holmes, Ben Farrelly, Noeley Cummins, Frankie Campbell, William Hayden

Kirby Club:
Jake Morton

Team Kehrer:
Klaus Kehrer, Katharina Stumpf, Erik Clewe, René Henoch, Martin Lutz, Alexa Becker, Ariane Braun, Barbara Karpf, Beate Kury, Tom Streicher, Alex Kunde, Daniel Sommer

And…The Core: Patrick, Lucien and Shep

With LOVE and THANKS to everyone for being in my corner.

Text: Bruce Weber
Image Processing: Kehrer Design (Erik Clewe, René Henoch)
Design: Kehrer Design (Katharina Stumpf)
Production: Kehrer Design (Thomas Streicher)

Front cover image: Alex. Training
Back cover image: Jamie S. Wirral Club
End paper (front): *Fight*, Lucien Frank

Joyce Carol Oates excerpts:
Oates, Joyce Carol *On Boxing*, Garden City, New York:
Dolphin/Doubleday, 1987. Print.
First Harper Perennial edition published 2006.
First quote: From the essay, *On Mike Tyson*, p. 138
Second Quote: *On Boxing*, page 4.

Printed and bound in Germany
ISBN 978-3-86828-632-8

Kehrer Heidelberg Berlin
www.kehrerverlag.com

BABY FACED ASSASSIN

Set in a port town outside of Liverpool, *Baby Faced Assassin* documents super-fly weight boxer Paul Butler as he prepares for his first title fight.

For information on exhibitions and screenings of *Baby Faced Assassin* please visit: www.jonafrank.com